JAMES BOND:
THE EVOLUTION OF BOND

1000 COPY LIMITED EDITION

DAMIEN M. BUCKLAND

Collection Editions Publishing 2015

JAMES BOND: THE EVOLUTION OF BOND

THIS SPECIAL EDITION BOOK IS LIMITED TO A MAXIMUM OF 1000 PAPERBACK COPIES WORLDWIDE

© DAMIEN BUCKLAND 2015

ALL RIGHTS RESERVED. NO PART OF THIS BOOK MAY BE REPRINTED OR REPRODUCED OR UTILIZED IN ANY FORM OR BY ANY ELECTRONIC, MECHANICAL, OR OTHER MEANS, NOW KNOWN OR HEREAFTER INVENTED, INCLUDING PHOTOCOPYING AND RECORDING, OR IN ANY INFORMATION STORAGE OR RETRIEVAL SYSTEM, WITHOUT PERMISSION IN WRITING FROM THE PUBLISHER OR AUTHOR.

THIS BOOK AND ITS AUTHOR IS IN NO WAY AFFILIATED WITH THE EON PRODUCTIONS OR THE FLEMING CORPORATION.. THE INFORMATION HELD HEREIN IS AVAILABLE TO PUBLIC DOMAIN AND ACTS SOLELY AS AN INFORMATIVE GUIDE PROVIDING A COMPREHENSIVE ILLUSTRATION OF THE JAMES FILMS AND FRANCHISE, ITS HISTORY, AND PROVIDING A PROMOTION OF THE JAMES BOND FRANCHISE. ALL PHOTOGRAPHS, PICTURES AND INFORMATION ARE RIGHTS PURCHASED OR ARE LISTED REUSE FOR COMMERCIAL USE.

ISBN-13: 978-1515009627

ISBN-10: 1515009629

Also by the Author:

TROJAN LAW FOR SECURITY OFFICERS (2013) (Retired)

LAW & PRACTICE FOR SECURITY PROFESSIONALS (2013)

COLLECTION EDITIONS: TOP GEAR (2014)

COLLECTION EDITIONS: NCIS (2014)

COLLECTION EDITIONS: MERCEDES IN FORMULA ONE (2014)

COLLECTION EDITIONS: GAME OF THRONES; An Inside Guide to the Hit Show (2014)

COLLECTION EDITIONS: SPACE SHUTTLE (2015)

COLLECTION EDITIONS: THE WALKING DEAD: Behind the Show (2015)

COLLECTION EDITIONS: FERRARI IN FORMULA ONE (2015)

TOP GEAR: 1977 – 2015 (2015)

Contents

AGENT 17F 7

ENTER HARRY & CUBBY 11

DR. NO 13

FROM RUSSIA WITH LOVE 19

GOLDFINGER 23

DISPUTE AND DEATH 26

THUNDERBALL 29

SIR JAMES BOND 33

YOU ONLY LIVE TWICE 37

ON HER MAJESTYS SECRET SERVICE 41

DIAMONDS ARE FOREVER 45

LIVE AND LET DIE 48

THE MAN WITH THE GOLDEN GUN 53

THE SPY WHO LOVED ME 57

MOONRAKER 62

FOR YOUR EYES ONLY 67

NEVER SAY NEVER AGAIN 72

OCTOPUSSY 75

A VIEW TO A KILL 79

SO CLOSE 81

THE LIVING DAYLIGHTS 83

LICENSE TO KILL 87

GOLDENEYE 92

TOMORROW NEVER DIES 97

THE WORLD IS NOT ENOUGH.. 101

DIE ANOTHER DAY 104

A NEW BREED 106

CASINO ROYALE 109

QUANTUM OF SOLACE 114

SKYFALL 120

SPECTRE 126

AGENT 17F

July, 1939… The outbreak of The Second World War. Rear Admiral John Godfrey, Director of Naval Intelligence, employs a Personal Assistant to work out of Room 39 of The Admiralty. This young Lieutenant has been commissioned into the Royal Naval Volunteer Reserve to work alongside Godfrey. His name is Ian Fleming but to all at the Admiralty, he would be known by his codename… "17F".

Despite a distinct lack of qualifications or experience for his new role, Fleming proved invaluable to Godfrey. Fleming showed a natural aptitude for administration and Godfrey soon promoted him to Commander and used Fleming as a liaison between his self and other sections of the wartime administration. Over the coming years, Fleming would continually prove himself to the wartime effort. In May of 1941, Fleming accompanied Admiral Godfrey to the U.S. where they assisted in writing the blueprint and plans for a new U.S department known as the "Office of the Coordinator of Information". This department later became the "Office of Strategic Services" and eventually what we would know of today as the "Central Intelligence Agency".

Later that year, Godfrey put Fleming in charge of "Operation Goldeneye". Goldeneye had been a plan to maintain an intelligence framework throughout Spain in the event of a German takeover of the territory. Fleming's plan involved maintaining communication with British held Gibraltar and launching sabotage operations against the Nazis from various bases there.

In 1942, Fleming formed a unit of commandos, known as No.30 Commando or 30 Assault Unit (30AU). These elite Commandos' composed of specialist intelligence troops whose job was to be near, or in front of, the front line of an advance and to seize enemy documents from previously targeted headquarters.

The success of 30 Assault Unit later led to a decision to establish a "Target Force", which became known as T-Force, in August of 1944. Fleming formed this elite group and the official memorandum, held at The National Archives in London, describes the unit's primary role as: "T-Force = Target Force, to guard and secure documents, persons, equipment, with combat and Intelligence personnel, after capture of large towns, ports etc. in liberated and enemy territory".

Fleming would sit on the committee that selected the targets for the T-Force unit, and listed them in the "Black Books" that were issued to the unit's officers. T-Force would head off rampaging across Europe digging out enemy secrets and finding adventure. Despite Fleming's natural aptitude as a leader, he secretly longed to be the man on the ground. One of the heroes he led rather than sitting in the relative comfort of headquarters leading from behind a desk.

Throughout the war Fleming had achieved significant success so by the end of the war he found himself lost with no real goal. His imagination had been stirred by his experiences during the Second World War and all that was left for him was as the Foreign Manager of the Kemsley Newspaper Group. His new role allowed Fleming to oversee the paper's worldwide network of correspondents but Fleming despised the job, bored by the dreariness and quiet of a newspaper office, he longed for adventure and paradise. On the far wall of his office he hung a rather faded framed picture of Montego Bay. Fleming's dream continued.

There was a positive side to Fleming's job at the newspaper office. His position allowed him to take three months leave each winter. Fleming, inspired by a trip to Jamaica during the war, bought a romantic hideaway there for the winter months. A house sat atop the beach with beautiful views across the ocean. Fleming named his new home "Goldeneye" and there he would spend his winter months swimming in the crisp, clear, oceans below.

Despite this new found paradise, Ian Fleming could never be a satisfied man. A woman could never be satisfying enough. A drink could never be good enough. The World is Not Enough could have been written especially to describe Fleming during these times. He needed something more, a new mission and as a new era approached with the outbreak of the Cold War, Fleming found something else to follow. Ian said "I am going to write the spy thriller to end all spy thrillers".

In his office at Goldeneye, Fleming closed the shutters and pulled a chair up to the desk in the corner of the room. Atop the desk sat a golden typewriter. Fleming sat at the desk and that day the world's greatest secret agent was born. But what to call this new hero? On the nearby bookcase sat a book titled "Birds of the West Indies" by author James Bond. Fleming looked over at this book and noticed the name of the author… Perfect… "I simply stole that and used it" (Ian Fleming).

As Casino Royale hit the bookshelves in 1953 critics, and even his wife, slammed it. Annie, Ian's wife, did not approve of the books and did not want the books to be dedicated to her. She thought the books were filth. Critics panned the "crude sadism" and "disgusting sex" with headlines such as "Fleming's Deadly Sin" and "Immoral Thug". It appeared that Fleming's imagination had been inspired too early and the 1950's public were simply not ready for such machoism.

Unperturbed, Fleming continued. He knew the book would make a great film and approached producers with the intention of selling the rights to make it a movie. Turned down almost every time, Fleming eventually sold the rights to Casino Royale for $1,000 to an American producer.

Casino Royale was turned into a one-hour television adventure. It was adapted for the screen by Anthony Ellis and Charles Bennett and the hour long episode aired on the 21st of October, 1954 and starred Barry Nelson as secret agent "Jimmy Bond" with Peter Lorre in the supporting role of "Le Chiffre". The character of Bond had been cast as an American Agent working for "Combined Intelligence" and was supported by a young British Agent known as "Clarence Leiter".

The show went largely unnoticed upon release. However, four years after the production of Casino Royale, CBS invited Fleming to write a further 32 episodes over a two-year period for a television show to be based upon the James Bond character. Fleming agreed and began to write outlines for this series. When nothing ever came of this, however, Fleming grouped and adapted three of the outlines into short stories and released the 1960 anthology For Your Eyes Only along with an additional two new short stories.

Producing the Bond books became a strain for Ian Fleming. He found it difficult to come up with new plots over the years. Fleming began to hit rock bottom and became desperate. He needed someone to come along and save Bond. At this same time, American film producer, Albert R. Broccoli (affectionately known as "Cubby") had picked up the Bond books. He was inspired by what drove Bond and why he acted as he did. Cubby immediately knew that he had to make Bond into a film and contacted Fleming to set up a meeting and discuss selling the rights to Bond. Luck was not on their side however. Shortly before the meeting, Cubby received the unfortunate news that his wife, Nedra, had been diagnosed with cancer. Cubby could not make the meeting but still intent on buying the rights to Bond, he sent his partner to the meeting instead. Cubby's partner was not a Bond fan though. The meeting went badly and Cubby's partner insulted Fleming by telling him that Bond was not film worthy material and instead would be better as a T.V show. Instead, in early 1960, Fleming sold the film rights to just one book, Casino Royale, for the measly sum of $6,000 to another film producer Charles K. Feldman but there was largely uncertainty over where this would end up, if anywhere. It was beginning to appear as if Bond would never hit the big screen.

ENTER HARRY & CUBBY

Fleming persisted. The books kept coming and in early 1961, excited by reading the novel Goldfinger, former Circus star and now Canadian film and theatre producer, Harry Saltzman bet every last penny he had to land the rights to James Bond. He won them but this left a dilemma... having spent everything obtaining the film rights, he had no money left to make the film. Saltzman was now in severe debt and had in his possession a gold mine that he just could not dig up alone.

Meanwhile, Cubby Broccoli had heard about Saltzman acquiring the rights and knew of his financial difficulties making the film. Cubby approached Saltzman and together they co-founded Danjaq, S.A. in 1962. Danjaq, S.A. became the holding company responsible for the copyright and trademarks of James Bond on screen, and the parent company of Eon Productions, which they also set up as a film production company for the Bond films. The moniker "Danjaq" was a combination of Broccoli's and Saltzman's wives' first names, Dana and Jacqueline.

Still more cash was needed though and so the pair got on a plane and flew to New York to convince production company Columbia to loan them the money to make a Bond film. Columbia turned Cubby and Saltzman down. Then United Artists stepped up. A meeting was set up and Cubby and Saltzman explained that they needed a million dollars up front for the film. In the 1960's, $1,000,000 was some serious cash for a film and a huge gamble for even United Artists but U.A. took the risk and agreed to funding the project. At last Bond was coming to the big screen.

Broccoli and Saltzman began a UK-wide search to cast Bond and held a "Find James Bond" contest to encourage auditions. The winner, Peter Anthony, won the role first but later dropped out due to stress. Patrick McGoohan, Richard Johnson, Rex Harrison, David Niven, Trevor Howard, and Broccoli's friend Cary Grant were all in contention at one point. Cary Grant was offered the role but he would only do one film and the plan was for several. James Mason was then offered the part but he said he would only do two films. So a little known Scottish actor landed the part instead. Sean Connery who had proven himself to both Cubby and Saltzman in his roles in On the Fiddle and the Little People. United Artists were not so satisfied however. U.A. wanted an American star to take the lead role and an almost unknown Scottish actor was not what they had envisioned.

Cubby and Saltzman continued to look but kept coming back to Connery. Eventually a screen test was filmed and shown to a largely female audience, the reaction was judged. Among the audience was Saltzman's wife. Afterwards he asked her, "was Connery sexy"? She responded "yes, are you kidding? He's very sexy"! The deal was clinched and Connery secured the role.

Next came the question of who would direct the film. Former tank commander, Terence Young was given that task. Broccoli had originally hired Richard Maibaum and Wolf Mankowitz to write Dr. No's screenplay. An initial draft of the screenplay was rejected. Mankowitz left the movie, and Maibaum undertook a second version, more closely in line with the novel this time. Johanna Harwood and thriller writer Berkely Mather worked on Maibaum's script.

DR. NO

On the 16th of January, 1962, filming commenced for the first Bond film, Dr. No, in Kingston, Jamaica. Shooting was only yards from Fleming's Goldeneye estate, fitting to be shot so close to where the character was born on paper. Locations filming took place largely in Oracabessa with further scenes shot at the Palisadoes strip and Port Royal in St. Andrew. One week later, the production left Jamaica with some footage still to be filmed there but prevented due to poor weather. Five days later, filming began again but this time at Pinewood Studios in Buckinghamshire, England. The sets were designed by Ken Adam and included Dr. No's base, the ventilation duct, and the interior of the British Secret Service Headquarters. The studio used for these scenes would in later years come to be known as the James Bond Studios.

Initial budget for the entire film was just £14,500 (equivalent to £276,272 in 2015), but Cubby and Saltzman were convinced to give over a further £6,000 out of their own finances.

The scene where a tarantula walks over Bond was initially shot by pinning a bed to the wall and placing Sean Connery over it, with a protective glass between him and the spider. Director Terence Young did not like the final results, so the scenes were interlaced with new footage featuring the tarantula over stuntman Bob Simmons. Simmons, who was un-credited for the film, described the scene as the most frightening stunt he had ever performed.

The original book also features a scene where Honey is tortured by being tied to the ground and surrounded by crabs. This proved difficult as the crabs were sent frozen from the Caribbean and so did not move very much, thus not giving quite the desired "scary" effect. Instead the film was altered to have Honey slowly drowning.

Bob Simmons also served as the film's fight choreographer, employing a rather rough fighting style for 1960's screen. The noted violence of Dr. No, which also included Bond shooting Dent in cold blood, caused producers to make adaptations in order to get an A-rating for the film and allowing minors to enter accompanied by an adult.

Also thrown into the film, when he is about to have dinner with Dr. No, Bond is amazed to see Goya's portrait of the Duke of Wellington. The painting had been stolen from the National Gallery by a 60 year-old amateur thief in London just weeks before filming began. Ken Adam had contacted the National Gallery in London to obtain a slide of the picture, painting the copy over the course of the weekend, prior to filming commencing on the Monday.

Title artist Maurice Binder, whilst creating the credits, had an idea for the introduction that would appear in all subsequent Bond films, the James Bond gun barrel sequence. It was filmed in sepia by putting a pinhole camera inside an actual .38 calibre gun barrel, with Bob Simmons playing Bond. Binder also designed a highly stylised main title sequence, a theme that has been repeated in the subsequent Eon-produced Bond films. Binder's budget for the entire title sequence was £2,000 (£38,106 in 2015).

As soon as late 1961 and with filming complete, United Artists started a marketing campaign to make James Bond a well-known name in North America. Newspapers received a box set of Bond's books, as well as a booklet detailing the Bond character and a picture of Ursula Andress. Eon and United Artists made licensing deals revolving around the character's tastes, having merchandising tie-ins with drink, tobacco, men's clothing and car companies. The campaign also focused on Ian Fleming's name due to the minor success of the books. After Dr. No had a successful run in Europe, Sean Connery and Terence Young did a cross-country tour in March 1963, which featured screening previews for the film and press conferences. It culminated in a well-publicized premiere in Kingston, where most of the film is set. Some of the campaign emphasized the sex appeal of the film, with the poster artwork, by Mitchell Hooks, depicting Sean Connery and four scantily clad women. The campaign also included the 007 logo designed by Joseph Caroff with a pistol as part of the seven.

Dr. No had its worldwide premiere at the London Pavilion, on the 5th of October, 1962, expanding to the rest of the United Kingdom three days later. The North American premiere, on the 8th of May, 1963, was more low-profile, with just 450 cinemas in Midwest and Southwest regions showing the film. On the 29th of May it opened in Los Angeles and at the same time it premiered in New York City as a double-bill alongside "The Young and the Brave".

In the United Kingdom, playing in 168 cinemas, Dr. No grossed $840,000 in just two weeks and wound up being the fifth most popular movie of the year there. The box office results in mainland Europe were just as good. The film ended up grossing $6 million, making it a financial success compared to its $1 million budget.

The film's North American release was not quite so fantastic to start off with. Upon release, Dr. No received a mixed critical reception. Time called Bond a "blithering bounder" and "a great big hairy marshmallow" who "almost always manages to seem slightly silly". Stanley Kauffmann in The New Republic said that he felt the film "never decides whether it is suspense or suspense-spoof." He also did not like Connery, or the Fleming novels. Even the Vatican condemned Dr. No because of Bond's cruelty and the sexual content, whilst the Kremlin said that Bond was the personification of capitalist evil. These negative reviews played in favour of the film though. Such poor recommendations from both the Kremlin and the Vatican only helped to increase public awareness of the film and thus greater cinema attendance.

In October of 1962, a comic book adaptation of the screenplay, written by Norman J. Nodel, was published in the United Kingdom as part of the Classics Illustrated anthology series. It was later reprinted in the United States by D.C Comics as part of its Showcase anthology series. It was one of the earliest comics to be censored on racial grounds (some skin tones and dialogue were changed for the American market).

The film version of Dr. No has many similarities to the novel and follows its basic plot, but there are a few notable omissions. Major elements from the novel that are missing from the film include Bond's fight with a giant squid, and the escape from Dr. No's complex using the dragon-disguised swamp buggy. Elements of the novel that were significantly changed for the film include the use of a (non-venomous) tarantula spider instead of a centipede; Dr. No's secret complex being disguised as a bauxite mine instead of a guano quarry; Dr. No's plot to disrupt NASA space launches from Cape Canaveral using a radio beam instead of disrupting US missile testing on Turks Island; the method of Dr. No's death by boiling in overheating reactor coolant rather than a burial under a chute of guano, and the introduction of SPECTRE, an organization absent from the book. Components absent from the novel but added to the film include the introduction of the Bond character in a gambling casino, the introduction of Bond's semi-regular girlfriend Sylvia Trench, a fight scene with an enemy chauffeur, a fight scene to introduce Quarrel, the seduction of Miss Taro, Bond's recurring CIA ally Felix Leiter, Dr. No's partner in crime Professor Dent and Bond's controversial cold-blooded killing of this character.

For the first Bond girl, Honey Ryder, Julie Christie was considered, but discarded as the producers felt she was not voluptuous enough. Just two weeks before filming began, Ursula Andress was chosen to play Honey after the producers saw a picture of her taken by Andress' then-husband John Derek. To appear more convincing as a Jamaican, Andress had a tan painted on her and ultimately had her voice dubbed over due to her heavy Swiss German accent. For Bond's antagonist Dr. No, Ian Fleming wanted his friend Noël Coward, and he answered the invitation with "No! No! No!" Fleming considered that his step-cousin, Christopher Lee, would be good for the role of Dr. No, although by the time Fleming told the producers, they had already chosen Joseph Wiseman for the part. Harry Saltzman picked Wiseman because of his performance in the 1951 film Detective Story, and the actor had special make-up applied to evoke Dr. No's supposed Chinese heritage.

The role as the first Felix Leiter was given to Jack Lord. This was Bond and Leiter's first time meeting each other on film and Leiter did not appear in the novel. This was Lord's only appearance as Leiter, as he asked for more money and a better billing to return as Leiter in Goldfinger and was subsequently replaced.

The cast also included a number of actors who were to become stalwarts of the future films, including Bernard Lee, who played Bond's superior M for another ten films, and Lois Maxwell, who played M's secretary Moneypenny in fourteen instalments of the series. Lee was chosen because of being a "prototypical father figure", and Maxwell after Fleming himself thought she was the perfect fit for his description of the character. Maxwell was initially offered a choice between the roles of Moneypenny or Sylvia Trench and opted for Moneypenny as she thought the Trench role, which included appearing in immodest dress, was too sexual. Eunice Gayson was cast as Sylvia Trench and it was planned that she would be a recurring girlfriend for Bond throughout six films, although she eventually appeared only in Dr. No and From Russia with Love. She had been given the part by director Terence Young, who had worked with her in Zarak and invited Gayson saying "You always bring me luck in my films".

One role which was not given to a future regular was that of Major Boothroyd, the head of Q-Branch, which was given to Peter Burton. Burton was unavailable for the subsequent film, From Russia with Love, and the role was taken by the much loved Desmond Llewelyn. Anthony Dawson, who played Professor Dent, met director Terence Young when he was working as a stage actor in London, but by the time of the film's shooting Dawson was working as a pilot and crop duster in Jamaica. Dawson also portrayed Ernst Stavro Blofeld, head of SPECTRE, in From Russia with Love and Thunderball, although his face was never seen and his voice was dubbed by Eric Pohlmann. The role of Taro was previously rejected by Marguerite LeWars, the Miss Jamaica 1961 who worked at the Kingston airport, as it required being "wrapped in a towel, lying in a bed, kissing a strange man". LeWars appeared as a photographer hired by Dr. No instead.

JAMES BOND IS BACK!

SEAN CONNERY as **JAMES BOND 007**

Albert R. Broccoli & Harry Saltzman Present

IAN FLEMING'S FROM RUSSIA WITH LOVE

FROM RUSSIA WITH LOVE

Following the success of Dr. No, United Artists not only agreed to fund a sequel but also doubled the first films budget as well as approving a bonus for Connery of $100,000 on top of his $54,000 salary.

By this time, Fleming's novels had picked up in popularity. President John F. Kennedy had named From Russia With Love amongst his favourite books and so Cubby and Saltzman decided that this would be the next film.

In addition to filming on location in Turkey, the action scenes were shot at Pinewood Studios and in Scotland. Production ran over budget and schedule, and the crew had to rush to finish by its scheduled October of 1963 release date.

Fleming's From Russia With Love novel was a Cold War thriller but the producers replaced the Soviet undercover agency SMERSH with the crime syndicate SPECTRE so as to avoid controversial political overtones. The SPECTRE training grounds were inspired by the film Spartacus. The original screenwriter had been Len Deighton, but he was replaced after a lack of progress. Thus, two of Dr. No's writers, Johanna Harwood and Richard Maibaum, returned for the second film in the series. Harwood stated in an interview in a Cinema Retro that she had been a screenwriter of several of Harry Saltzman's projects, and her screenplay for From Russia with Love had followed Fleming's novel closely, but she left the film early due to what she called Terence Young's constant rewriting of her screenplay with ideas that were not in the original Fleming work.

Although uncredited, the actor who played Number 1 was Anthony Dawson, who had played Professor Dent in Dr. No. In the end credits, Blofeld is credited with a "?". Blofeld's voice was provided by Viennese actor Eric Pohlmann and Peter Burton was unavailable to return as Major Boothroyd, so Desmond Llewelyn accepted the part. However, screen credit for Llewelyn was omitted at the opening of the film and is reserved for the exit credits, where he is credited simply as "Boothroyd". Llewelyn's character was not referred to by this name in dialogue, but M does introduce him as being from Q Branch. Llewelyn would remain as the character, better known as Q, in all but two of the series' films until his death in 1999.

For the role of Tatiana, a number of actresses were considered including Sylva Koscina, Annette Vadim, Virna Lisi, but the part finally went to the 1960 Miss Universe runner-up, Daniela Bianchi, supposedly at the request of Connery. Daniela's English was limited and she started taking English classes prior to filming but the studios decided ultimately to dub her voice for the film.

Terence Young cast Lotte Lenya in the role of Rosa Klebb after hearing one of her musical recordings. Young wanted Kronsteen's portrayer to be "an actor with a remarkable face", so the minor character would be well remembered by audiences. This led to the casting of Vladek Sheybal, who Young also considered convincing as an intellectual. Several women were tested for the roles of Vida and Zora, the two fighting Gypsy girls, and after Aliza Gur and Martine Beswick were cast, they spent six weeks practicing their fight choreography with stunt work arranger Peter Perkins.

For the part of Kerim Bey, Pedro Armendáriz was recommended to Young by director John Ford. After experiencing increasing discomfort on location in Istanbul, Armendáriz was diagnosed with inoperable cancer. Filming in Istanbul was terminated and the production moved to Britain. Armendáriz's scenes were brought forward so that he could complete his scenes without delay. Though visibly in pain, he continued working as long as possible. When he could no longer work, he returned home and took his own life. Remaining shots after Armendáriz left London used a stunt double and Terence Young himself as stand-ins.

Most of the film was set in Istanbul, Turkey. Other locations included the Basilica Cistern, Hagia Sophia, and the Sirkeci Station which also was used for the Belgrade and Zagreb railway stations. The MI6 office in London, SPECTRE Island, the Venice hotel and the interior scenes of the Orient Express were filmed at Pinewood Studios with some footage of the train. In the film, the train journey was set in Eastern Europe. The journey and the truck ride were shot in Argyll, Scotland and Switzerland. The end scenes for the film were shot in Venice however, to qualify for the British film funding of the time, which the movie had taken, at least 70 percent of the film had to have been filmed in Great Britain or the Commonwealth so the Gypsy camp was also to be filmed in an actual camp in Topkapi, but was actually shot in a replica of it in Pinewood. The scene with rats (after the theft of the Lektor) was shot in Spain, as Britain did not allow filming with wild rats, and filming white rats painted in cocoa did not work.

Director Terence Young's eye for realism was evident throughout production. For the opening chess match, Kronsteen wins the game with a re-enactment of Boris Spassky's victory over David Bronstein in 1960. Production Designer Syd Cain built up the "chess pawn" motif in his $150,000 set for the brief sequence. A noteworthy gadget featured was the attaché case issued by Q Branch. It had a tear gas bomb that detonated if the case was improperly opened, a folding AR-7 Sniper Rifle with twenty rounds of ammunition, a throwing knife, and 50 gold sovereigns.

The shoot suffered further bad luck. It was behind schedule and over-budget, the production crew struggled to complete production in time for the already-announced premiere date of that October. On the 6th of July, 1963, while scouting locations in Argyll, Scotland for that day's filming of the climactic boat chase, Terence Young's helicopter crashed into the water with art director Michael White and a cameraman aboard. The craft sank into 40–50 feet (12–15 m) of water, but all escaped with minor injuries. Despite the calamity, Young was behind the camera for the full day's work. A few days later, Bianchi's driver fell asleep during the commute to a 6 am shoot and crashed the car. Bianchi's face was bruised, and her scenes had to be delayed two weeks while these facial contusions healed.

The helicopter and boat chase scenes were not in the original novel, but were added to create an action climax. These two scenes would initially be shot in Istanbul, but were moved to Scotland. The speed-boats could not run fast enough due to the choppy seas, and a rented boat filled with cameras ended up sinking in the Bosphorus. A helicopter was also hard to obtain, the special effects crew were nearly arrested trying to get one at a local air base. The helicopter chase ended up being filmed with a radio controlled miniature helicopter and the explosion, shot in Pinewood, got out of control, burning Walter Gotell's eyelids and seriously injuring three stuntmen.

For the opening credits, Maurice Binder had disagreements with the producers and did not want to return. Instead, designer Robert Brownjohn stepped into his place, and projected the credits on female dancers. He had been inspired by constructivist artist Laszlo Moholy-Nagy projecting light onto clouds in the 1920s. Brownjohn's work started the tradition of scantily clad women in the Bond films' title sequences for all future films.

On the 10th of October, 1963, at the Odeon Leicester Square in London From Russia With Love had its U.K. premiere. The following year, it was released in 16 further countries worldwide, with the United States premiere on the 8th of April, 1964, at New York's Astor Theatre. Upon its first release, From Russia with Love doubled Dr. No's gross by earning $12.5 million ($95 million in 2015 dollars) at the worldwide box office. After reissue it grossed $78 million, of which $24 million was from North America. Bond had become a success.

JAMES BOND IS BACK IN ACTION!
EVERYTHING HE TOUCHES
TURNS TO EXCITEMENT!!!
ALBERT R. BROCCOLI and HARRY SALTZMAN present
SEAN CONNERY AS AGENT 007
in IAN FLEMING'S "GOLDFINGER"
TECHNICOLOR
STARRING
GERT FROBE as GOLDFINGER
HONOR BLACKMAN as PUSSY GALORE
ALSO STARRING
SHIRLEY EATON
SCREENPLAY BY
RICHARD MAIBAUM and PAUL DEHN
PRODUCED BY
HARRY SALTZMAN and ALBERT R. BROCCOLI
DIRECTED BY GUY HAMILTON
RELEASED THRU
UNITED ARTISTS

GOLDFINGER

Albert R. Broccoli and Harry Saltzman turned to Goldfinger as the third Bond film. Goldfinger had a massive budget compared to the previous two films at $3 million, the equivalent of the budgets of Dr. No and From Russia With Love combined. To recoup such a large budget, Goldfinger was chosen with the American cinema market in mind, as the previous films had concentrated on the Caribbean and European theatre.

Terence Young, who directed the previous two films, chose to film The Amorous Adventures of Moll Flanders instead, after a pay dispute that saw him denied a percentage of the film's profits. Broccoli and Saltzman turned instead to Guy Hamilton to direct.

Richard Maibaum, who wrote the previous films, returned to adapt the seventh James Bond novel. Maibaum fixed the novel's heavily criticized plot hole, where Goldfinger actually attempts to empty Fort Knox. In the film, Bond notes it would take twelve days for Goldfinger to steal the gold, before the villain reveals he actually intends to irradiate it with the then topical concept of a Red Chinese Atomic Bomb. However, Harry Saltzman disliked the first draft, and brought in Paul Dehn to revise it. Hamilton said Dehn "brought out the British side of things" but Connery disliked his draft, so Maibaum returned. Dehn also suggested the pre-credit sequence to be an action scene with no relevance to the actual plot. Something which continues to this day.

Principle photography on Goldfinger begun on the 20th of January, 1964, in Miami, Florida, at the Fontainebleau Hotel. The crew was small, consisting only of Hamilton, Broccoli, Adam, and cinematographer Ted Moore. Sean Connery could not get to Florida to film Goldfinger because he was filming another film, Marnie, elsewhere in the United States.

After five days in Florida, production moved to England. The primary location was, of course, Pinewood Studios, home to among other sets, a recreation of the Fontainebleau, the South American city of the pre-title sequence and both Goldfinger's estate and factory. Three places near the studio were used, Black Park for the car chase involving Bond's Aston Martin and Goldfinger's henchmen inside the factory complex, RAF Northolt for the American airports and Stoke Park Club for the golf club scene. The end of the chase, when Bond's

Aston Martin crashes into a wall because of the mirror and the chase immediately preceding it, were filmed on the road at the rear of Pinewood Studios Sound Stages A and E and the Prop Store. The road is now called Goldfinger Avenue. Southend Airport was used for the scene where Goldfinger flies to Switzerland. The second unit filmed in Kentucky, and these shots were edited into scenes filmed at Pinewood. Principal photography then moved to Switzerland, with the car chase being filmed at the small curves roads near Realp, the exterior of the Pilatus Aircraft factory in Stans serving as Goldfinger's factory, and Tilly Masterson's attempt to snipe Goldfinger being shot in the Furka Pass.

Goldfinger also debuted one of Bond's most famous gadgets. The Aston Martin DB5. Getting the car for filming was not that easy though. When Saltzman and Cubby approached Aston Martin and asked if they could "have" a couple of DB5's for their movie, Aston turned around and said "No… Absolutely not".

Saltzman came back at them and Aston Martin again said "No! But we will sell you one… at the full price… £4,500". At this point Saltzman slammed the phone down and the world's most famous car was on the verge of becoming a Jaguar. A Jenson and a Chevrolet were also considered but Bond producers kept plugging away at Aston Martin. Finally, Aston begrudgingly loaned them a second hand development car. The car was "gadgetised" by special effects at a cost of £25,000. More than five times the price of buying the actual car. Not all the cars gadgets were that high tech though. The smoke screen from the rear of the car was actually a very small prop man hidden in the boot. A hole was cut in the rear of the car and all he had to do was light the canister and hold it out of the hole. Problem was that there was a hole in the canister and the smoke filled up the boot. The prop man was almost suffocated in the back of the car but the effect worked.

Broccoli earned permission to film in the Fort Knox area with the help of his friend, Lt. Colonel Charles Russhon. To shoot Pussy Galore's Flying Circus gassing the soldiers, the pilots were only allowed to fly above 3000 feet. Hamilton later recalled this was "hopeless", so they flew at about 500 feet, "and the military went absolutely ape". The scenes of people fainting involved the same set of soldiers moving to different locations. For security reasons, the filmmakers were not allowed to film inside the Bullion Depository, although exterior photography was permitted. All sets for the interiors of the building were designed and built from scratch at Pinewood Studios. The filmmakers had no clue as to what the interior of the depository looked like, so Ken Adam's imagination provided the idea of gold stacked upon gold behind iron bars. Saltzman disliked the design's resemblance to a prison, but Hamilton liked it enough that it was built.

Filming wrapped up on the 11th of July in Andermatt, after nineteen weeks of shooting. At Leicester Square in London on the 17th of September, 1964, Goldfinger came to the screen.

Crowds in Leicester Square that evening were in such numbers that Police were unable to control the numbers. The glass doors at the front of the cinema were accidentally broken as the number of people hoping for a glimpse of the stars grew and pushed against the front of the building. Three months later, on the 21st of December, Goldfinger opened in the U.S. showing across 41 cities and peaking on 485 screens at one point. The film's success continued to expand worldwide, with the exception of Israel. Here the film was banned when it became known that Gert Fröbe (the actor portraying Auric Goldfinger) had once been connected to the Nazi Party. Many years later the ban was lifted when a Jewish family who had survived persecution during the Second World War stepped forward and publicly thanked Gert Fröbe. Gert had joined the Nazi Party in 1929, when he was just 16, in his home town of Oberplanitz (Zwickau today). By 1937, he had left the party and during the Nazi Party's reign Gert had aided in hiding German Jews and protecting them from the Gestapo. The family that had thanked him had been just one of those he had helped to save during the war.

Goldfinger was such a success that it recouped its original $3 million budget in just two weeks and broke box office records in multiple countries around the world. The Guinness Book of Records listed Goldfinger as the fastest grossing film of all time and one cinema (the DeMille in New York City) opened its doors 24 hours a day to keep up with demand to see the film. As the film's original box office run closed it had grossed more than $23 million in the U.S. and $46 million worldwide. In 1966, Goldfinger was reissued as a double bill alongside Dr. No. Goldfinger grossed a total of $51,081,062 in the United States and $73,800,000 elsewhere, for a total worldwide gross of $124,900,000.

DISPUTE AND DEATH

As the Bond name grew so did the reputations of Eon Productions. Broccoli and Saltzman had more money than they had ever had before and both began to live the celebrity lifestyles themselves. Unfortunately, despite increasing book sales, the success of Bond did not always benefit Ian Fleming. Fleming had gone through a High Court ordeal against a man named Kevin McClory.

Before Bond had come to the screen, McClory and Fleming had collaborated on scripting an underwater Bond adventure (which would later become the genesis for Thunderball). As the Thunderball book was released, McClory had taken legal action against Fleming for Plagiarism. He claimed that the original idea had come from him and Fleming claimed it had been his. In reality the pair had spent their time drinking in Jamaica and devising the story together. Neither of them was likely to remember who had come up with which part of the story.

The dispute continued however, and the claim was eventually settled out of court with McClory winning the rights to make the Thunderball movie just at the time that Eon Productions had planned to make the film themselves. McClory had wanted to make the film himself but neither Cubby nor Harry wanted to see an independent Bond on the screen fearing that it could destroy the brand. Instead, Broccoli and Saltzman got together with McClory and agreed to cinematically adapt the novel between them. The conditions demanded by McClory were that he would be sole Producer of the film with Broccoli and Saltzman as Executive Producers. He also kept ownership to the film rights on Thunderball and made it clear that in future years he would have the right to remake the film in any way he saw best. This final demand gave rise to all of the problems which would come in later years.

Meanwhile, the High Court action and the dispute over Thunderball had taken its toll on Fleming. He had already suffered one heart attack back in 1961 and on August the 11th, 1964, whilst staying at a hotel in Canterbury Fleming collapsed after a meal with friends. He had suffered a second heart attack. His last words were to the ambulance drivers… "I am sorry to trouble you chaps. I don't know how you get along so fast with the traffic on the roads these days". In the early hours of August the 12th, Fleming passed away, only weeks before the release of Goldfinger to the screen. He had written two further Bond books, "The Man with the Golden Gun" and another Bond book featuring two short stories, "Octopussy and The Living Daylights". Neither book had yet reached the bookshelves and both were later published posthumously.

LOO7K UP!
LOO7K DOWN!
LOO7K OUT!
HERE COMES THE BIGGEST BOND OF ALL!
SEAN CONNERY
"THUNDERBALL"
PANAVISION TECHNICOLOR
UNITED ARTISTS

THUNDERBALL

Filming for Thunderball commenced on the 16th of February, 1965, with principal photography of the opening scene shot in Paris. Filming then moved to the Château d'Anet, near Dreux, France, for the fight in pre-credit sequence.

Filming also took place at Pinewood Studios, Buckinghamshire, Silverstone racing circuit for the chase involving Count Lippe, Fiona Volpe and James Bond's DB5 before moving to Nassau, and Paradise Island in The Bahamas (where most of the footage was shot), and Miami. Huntington Hartford gave permission to shoot footage on his Paradise Island and is thanked at the end of the movie.

On arriving in Nassau, McClory searched for possible locations to shoot many of the key sequences of the film and used the home of a local millionaire couple, the Sullivan's, for Largo's estate. Part of the SPECTRE underwater assault was also shot on the coastal grounds of another millionaires' home on the island. The most difficult sequences to film were the underwater action scenes and the first to be shot underwater was at a depth of 50 feet to shoot the scene where SPECTRE divers remove the atomic bombs from the sunken Vulcan bomber. Peter Lamont had previously visited a Royal Air Force bomber station carrying a concealed camera which he used to get close-up shots of the secretive missiles and those appearing in the film were not actually present. Most of the underwater scenes had to be done at lower tides due to the sharks in the Bahamian sea.

Connery's was wary of scenes involving the use of sharks, such as the scene where Bond is trapped in a shark-infested pool. He insisted that Ken Adam build a special Plexiglas partition inside the pool but, despite this, it was not a fixed structure and one of the sharks managed to pass through it; forcing Connery to abandon the pool immediately. Another dangerous situation occurred when special effects coordinator John Stears brought in a supposed dead shark carcass to be towed around the pool. The shark, however, was not dead and revived at one point. Due to the increasing dangers and mishaps on the set, stuntman Bill Cummings demanded an extra fee £250 to double for Largo's sidekick Quist as he was dropped into the pool of sharks.

The climactic underwater battle was shot at Clifton Pier and was choreographed by Hollywood expert Ricou Browning, who had worked on many films previously such as Creature from the Black Lagoon in 1954. He was responsible for the staging of the cave sequence and the battle scenes beneath the Disco Volante and called in his specialist team of divers who posed as those engaged in the onslaught. Voit provided much of the underwater gear in exchange for product placement and film tie-in merchandise. Lamar Boren, an underwater photographer, was brought in to shoot all of the sequences. United States Air Force Lieutenant-Colonel Charles Russhon, who had already helped alliance Eon productions with the local authorities in Turkey for From Russia With Love (1963) and at Fort Knox for Goldfinger (1964), using his position, was able to gain access to the United States Navy's Fulton surface-to-air recovery system, used to lift Bond and Domino from the water at the end of the film. He was also able to supply the experimental rocket fuel used to destroy the Disco Volante. During the final days shooting, special effects supervisor John Stears was using this experimental rocket fuel for use in exploding Largo's yacht, the Disco Volante. Ignoring the true power of the volatile liquid, Stears doused the entire yacht with it, took cover, and then detonated the boat. The resultant massive explosion shattered windows along Bay Street in Nassau roughly 30 miles away. Stears went on to win an Academy Award for his work on Thunderball.

Filming ceased in May 1965 and the final scene shot was the physical fight on the bridge of the Disco Volante.

As the filming neared its conclusion, Connery had become increasingly agitated with press intrusion and was distracted with difficulties in his marriage of 32 months to actress Diane Cilento. Connery refused to speak to journalists and photographers who followed him in Nassau stating his frustration with the harassment that came with the role;

"I find that fame tends to turn one from an actor and a human being into a piece of merchandise, a public institution. Well, I don't intend to undergo that metamorphosis."

In the end he only gave a single interview to Playboy as filming was wrapped up, and even turned down a substantial fee to appear in a promotional TV special made by Wolper Productions for NBC called The Incredible World of James Bond.

Thunderball premiered on the 9th of December, 1965, in Tokyo and opened on the 29th of December, 1965, in the UK. It was a major success at the box office with record-breaking earnings and became the highest grossing Bond film to date with a net profit of $26,500,000. It eventually grossed $63.6 million in the United States, equating to roughly 58.1 million admissions. In total, the film has earned $141.2 million worldwide, surpassing the earnings of the three preceding films in the series and easily recouping its $9 million budget. It remained the highest-grossing Bond film until Live and Let Die in 1973.

With the end of Thunderball, Sean Connery had started to have reservations about the role and the future of the James Bond film franchise. In February of 1965 Connery was quoted in The Daily Mail saying,

> *"I think it could be better than the last one, but I can't see the cycle going on past that. Though I am signed to do two more - OHMSS and one other. But who knows? America seems to lap them up... My only grumble about the Bond films is that they don't tax one as an actor... I'd like to see someone else tackle Bond, I must say - though I think they'd be crazy to do it."*

JAMES BOND 007

"CASINO ROYALE"

CASINO ROYALE

¡ ES DEMASIADO PARA UN SOLO JAMES BOND!

PANTALLA GIGANTE
SUPERPANORAMA 70 m/m

TECHNICOLOR PETER SELLERS · URSULA ANDRESS · DAVID NIVEN
WOODY ALLEN · JOANNA PETTET · ORSON WELLES · DALIAH LAVI · DEBORAH KERR
WILLIAM HOLDEN · CHARLES BOYER · GEORGE RAFT · JOHN HUSTON · TERENCE COOPER
BARBARA BOUCHET

PRODUCIDA POR CHARLES K FELDMAN y JERRY BRESLER · DIRIGIDA POR JOHN HUSTON, KEN HUGHES, VAL GUEST, ROBERT PARRISH, JOE McGRATH · SEGUN LA NOVELA DE IAN FLEMING

SIR JAMES BOND

Way back in March of 1955, before Ian Fleming had met Cubby Broccoli or Harry Saltzman, Fleming had sold the film rights of his novel Casino Royale, the first book featuring the character of James Bond, to the producer Gregory Ratoff for $6,000. The following year Ratoff set up a production company with Michael Garrison to produce a film adaptation of the novel, but wound up not finding the financial backers before his death in December of 1960. After Ratoff's death, the producer Charles K. Feldman represented Ratoff's widow and obtained the Casino Royale rights from her. Albert R. Broccoli, who had a long time interest in adapting James Bond, offered to purchase the Casino Royale rights from Feldman, but he declined. Feldman and his friend, the director Howard Hawks, had wanted to adapt Casino Royale themselves, considering Leigh Brackett as a writer and Cary Grant as James Bond. The idea was eventually shelved in 1962 with the release of Eon's Dr. No, but by 1964, with Feldman having invested nearly $550,000 of his own money into pre-production of Casino Royale, he decided to go back to Eon and United Artists and try a deal. The attempt at a co-production eventually fell through as Feldman frequently argued with Broccoli and Saltzman, especially regarding the profit divisions and when the Casino Royale adaptation would start production. Feldman approached Sean Connery to play Bond, and he said yes… for one million dollars, which Feldman certainly could not afford. Feldman eventually decided to offer his project to Columbia Pictures through a script written by Ben Hecht, and the studio accepted. The problem was that the success of Eon's James Bond had started a spy film craze. Other production companies were beginning to make spy films and T.V shows and Feldman needed something different and so he opted to make his film a spoof of the Bond series instead of a straightforward adaptation.

The principal filming was carried out at Pinewood Studios, Shepperton Studios, and Twickenham Studios with extensive sequences also featuring various areas of London, notably Trafalgar Square and the exterior of 10 Downing Street. Mereworth Castle in Kent was used as the home of 'Sir' James Bond, which is blown up at the start of the film. Much of the filming for M's Scottish castle was actually done on location in County Meath, Ireland, with Killeen Castle, Dunsany, as the focus. However the car chase sequences where Bond leaves the castle were shot in the Perthshire village of Killin.

The production proved to be rather troubled, with five different directors helming various different segments of the film, with stunt coordinator Richard Talmadge co-directing the final sequence. In addition to the credited writers, Woody Allen, Peter Sellers, Val Guest, Ben Hecht, Joseph Heller, Terry Southern, and Billy Wilder are all believed to have contributed to the screenplay to varying degrees. Val Guest was given the responsibility of splicing the various "chapters" together, and was offered the unique title of "Coordinating Director" but declined, claiming the chaotic plot would not reflect well on him if he were so credited. His extra credit was labelled "Additional Sequences" instead.

Part of the behind-the-scenes drama of this film's production concerned the filming of the segments involving Peter Sellers. Screenwriter Wolf Mankowitz declared that Sellers felt intimidated by Orson Welles to the extent that, except for a couple of shots, neither was in the studio simultaneously. Other versions of the legend depict the drama stemming from Sellers being slighted, in favour of Welles, by Princess Margaret during her visit to the set. Welles also insisted on performing magic tricks as Le Chiffre, and the director obliged. Director Val Guest wrote that Welles did not think much of Sellers, and had refused to work with "that amateur". Director Joseph McGrath, a personal friend of Sellers, was punched by the actor when he complained about Sellers' behaviour on the set.

Sellers left the production before all his scenes were shot, which is why Tremble is so abruptly captured in the film. Whether he was fired or simply walked off is unclear. Given that he often went absent for days at a time and was involved in conflicts with Welles, either explanation is plausible. Regardless, Sellers was unavailable for the filming of an ending and of linking footage to explain the details, leaving the filmmakers to devise a way to make the existing footage work without him. The framing device of a beginning and ending with David Niven was invented to salvage the footage. Val Guest indicated that he was given the task of creating a narrative thread which would link all segments of the film. He chose to use the original Bond and Vesper as linking characters to tie the story together. Guest states that in the originally released versions of the film, a cardboard cut-out of Sellers in the background was used for the final scenes. In later versions, this cardboard cut-out image was replaced by a sequence showing Sellers in highland dress, inserted by "trick photography".

Signs of missing footage from the Sellers segments are evident at various points. Evelyn Tremble is not captured on camera, an outtake of Sellers entering a racing car was substituted. In this outtake, Sellers calls for the car, à la Pink Panther, to chase down Vesper and her kidnappers; the next thing that is shown is Tremble being tortured. Out-takes of Sellers were also used for Tremble's dream sequence (pretending to play the piano on Ursula Andres's torso), in the finale (blowing out the candles whilst in highland dress) and at the end of the film when all the various

"James Bond doubles" are together. In the kidnap sequence, Tremble's death is also very abruptly inserted; it consists of pre-existing footage of Sellers being rescued by Vesper, followed by a later-filmed shot of her abruptly deciding to shoot Tremble, followed by a freeze-frame over some of the previous footage of her surrounded by bodies (noticeably a zoom-in on the previous shot).

As well as this, an entire sequence involving Tremble going to the front for the underground James Bond Training School (which turns out to be under Harrods, of which the training area was the lowest level) was never shot, thus creating an abrupt cut from Vesper announcing that Tremble will be James Bond to Tremble exiting the elevator into the Training School.

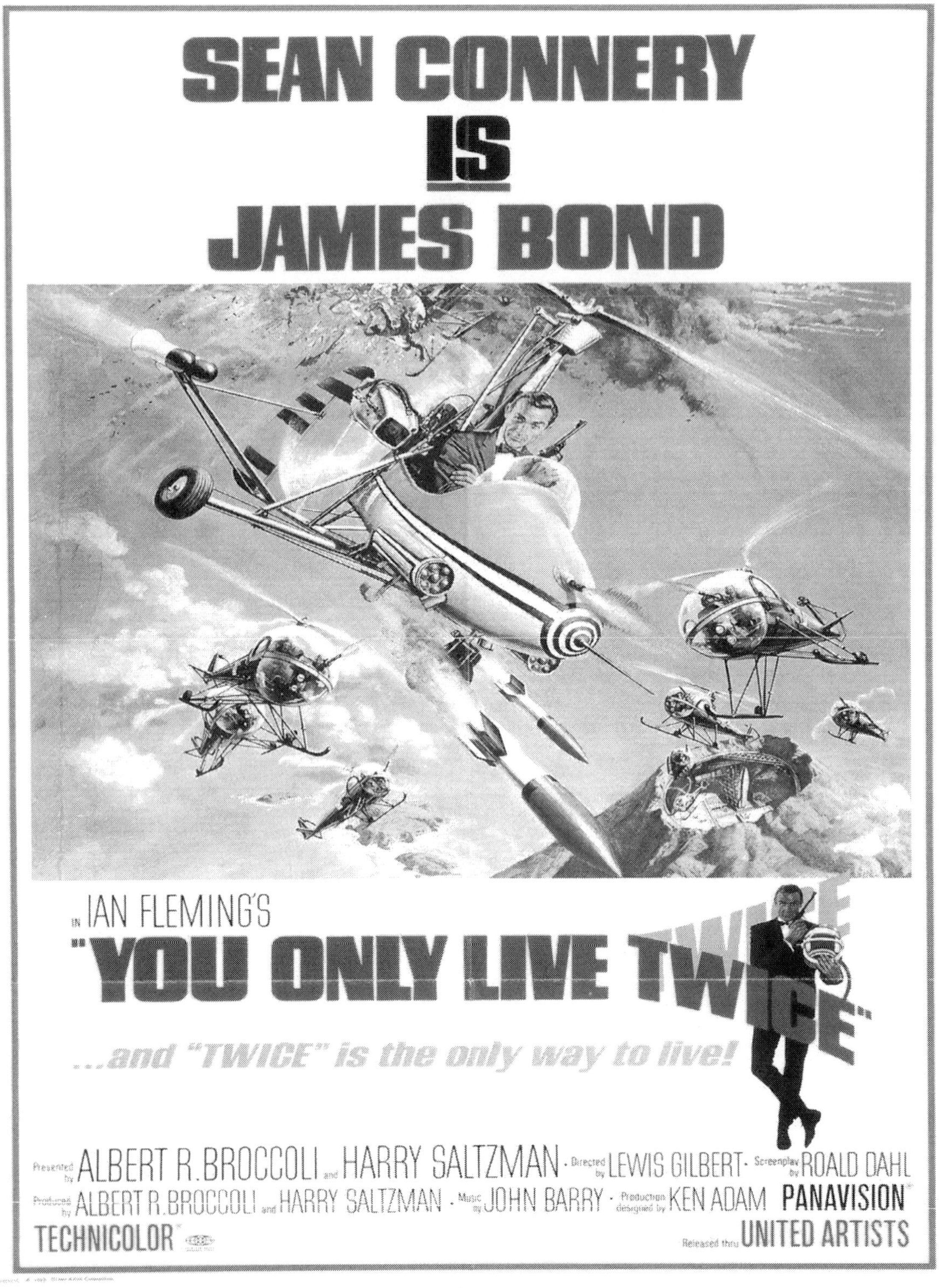

"YOU ONLY LIVE TWICE"

YOU ONLY LIVE TWICE

The next Eon Bond movie planned was On Her Majesty's Secret Service but at the last minute it was decided to adapt You Only Live Twice instead as there had been issues with searching for locations suitable for OHMSS. Director Lewis Gilbert, Albert R. Broccoli, Harry Saltzman, Production Designer Ken Adam, and Director of Photography Freddie Young, flew to Japan. Together they spent three weeks searching for suitable locations. In Fleming's novel, SPECTRE's hideout was a shore fortress. For the film this was changed to an extinct volcano after it became apparent that the Japanese in fact did not make castles. The location team had been due to fly back to the U.K. aboard BOAC Flight 911 on the 5th of March, 1966, but skipped the flight to watch a Ninja demonstration to see if it could have a place in the film. The flight they had been due on crashed 25 minutes after take-off killing everyone on board.

The producers had Harold Jack Bloom come to Japan with them to write a screenplay. Bloom's work was ultimately rejected, but since several of his ideas were used in the final script, Bloom was given the credit of "Additional Story Material". Among the elements were the opening with Bond's fake death and burial at sea, and the ninja attack. As the screenwriter of the previous Bond films Richard Maibaum was unavailable, Roald Dahl, close friend of Ian Fleming and children's book author, was chosen to write the adaptation despite having no prior experience writing a screenplay except for the uncompleted The Bells of Hell Go Ting-a-ling-a-ling.

Dahl said the original novel was "Ian Fleming's worst book, with no plot in it which would even make a movie", and compared it to a travelogue, and said he had to create a new plot. On creating the plot, Dahl said he "didn't know what the hell Bond was going to do" despite having to deliver the first draft in six weeks, and decided to do a basic plot similar to Dr. No. Dahl was given a free rein on his script, except for the character of Bond and "the girl formula", involving three women for Bond to seduce including an ally and a henchwoman who both get killed, and the main Bond girl. While the third involved a character from the book, Kissy Suzuki, Dahl had to create Aki and Helga Brandt to fulfil the rest.

Filming of You Only Live Twice lasted from July of 1966 to March of 1967. The film was shot primarily in Japan. Hyōgo was depicted as Tanaka's ninja training camp. His private transportation hub was filmed at the Tokyo Metro's Nakano-shimbashi Station. The Hotel New Otani in Tokyo served as the outside for Osato Chemicals and the hotel's gardens were used for scenes of the ninja training. Bōnotsu in Kagoshima served as the fishing village, the Kobe Harbour was used for the dock fight and Mount Shinmoe-dake in Kyūshū was used for the exteriors of SPECTRE's headquarters.

The heavily armed WA-116 autogyro "Little Nellie" was included after Ken Adam heard a radio interview with its inventor, RAF Wing Commander Ken Wallis. Little Nellie was named after music hall star Nellie Wallace, who has a similar surname to its inventor. Wallis piloted his invention, which was equipped with various mock-up armaments by John Stears' special effects team, during production. "Nellie's" battle with helicopters proved to be difficult to film. The scenes were initially shot in Miyazaki, first with takes of the gyrocopter, with more than 85 take-offs, 5 hours of flight and Wallis nearly crashing into the camera several times. A scene filming the helicopters from above created a major downdraft and cameraman John Jordan's foot was severed by the craft's rotor. The concluding shots involved explosions, which the Japanese government did not allow in a national park. So, the crew moved to Torremolinos, Spain, which was found to resemble the Japanese landscape. The sets of SPECTRE's volcano base were constructed at a lot inside Pinewood Studios, with a cost of $1 million and including operative heliport and monorail.

Since the majority of You Only Live Twice was set in Japan, a Japanese car would have to be used for Connery. After negotiations with Toyota a 2000GT was chosen. Toyota supplied the car and as it was delivered to the studios at Pinewood, and with only two weeks to filming, a problem became apparent. The 2000GT is a sports car and as such is quite low down. Sean Connery on the other hand is not at 6'2" tall. When Sean sat in the car his head was bent at an angle. He simply would not fit. The solution was a convertible but Toyota did not make convertible versions of this car. Still, Toyota came up trumps. They collected the car and returned it just in time for filming with the top chopped off. The 2000GT for Bond was now a convertible. A tonneau cover was fitted to the rear of the car to give the appearance that it had a fold down roof.

You Only Live Twice also provided a major turning point in the Bond franchise. Sean Connery's success and fame had got to him. No matter how much money he was offered he would always feel it was not enough. Sean felt that he was being exploited and became resentful towards the film's creators for this. The relationship especially between Saltzman and Connery neared breaking point. They both began to hate the sight of each other and at one point, on the set of You Only Live Twice, Harry walked on stage. Connery stopped mid-dialogue. He just stood there without saying a word. The crew looked on in puzzlement wondering what had happened when suddenly they could see Harry stood to the side. Sean turned to him and said "if you ever walk on the stage again, I will stop work". Saltzman and Broccoli appeared to have created a monster.

Tensions during filming continued and Connery eventually told United Artists that he would not be fulfilling the remainder of his contract and would make You Only Live Twice his final Bond film. Sean was gone… He was out and United Artists were shocked, but Saltzman and Broccoli both felt that James Bond was bigger than the actor that portrayed him. They knew the success could continue with a new Bond and the game was not over.

FAR UP! FAR OUT! FAR MORE!
James Bond 007 is back!

ALBERT R. BROCCOLI
AND
HARRY SALTZMAN
present

JAMES BOND 007
in IAN FLEMING'S
"ON HER MAJESTY'S SECRET SERVICE"

starring GEORGE LAZENBY · DIANA RIGG · TELLY SAVALAS as Blofeld
also starring GABRIELE FERZETTI and ILSE STEPPAT · Produced by ALBERT R. BROCCOLI and HARRY SALTZMAN
Directed by PETER HUNT · Screenplay by RICHARD MAIBAUM · Music by JOHN BARRY · PANAVISION® · TECHNICOLOR® United Artists

ORIGINAL MOTION PICTURE SOUNDTRACK ALBUM BY JOHN BARRY AVAILABLE ON UNITED ARTISTS RECORDS

ON HER MAJESTYS SECRET SERVICE

Back in 1962, a young George Lazenby had taken a girl to see the release of Dr. No. By the end of the film he knew that he wanted to be Bond more than anything and had set his sights on the role despite not actually being an actor and having absolutely no acting experience whatsoever.

With the departure of Connery and the search for a new Bond on a few years later, George saw his opportunity. He went to the tailors and brought a suit that Connery had not wanted. He brought a Rolex watch. George even went to Connery's barber and got a new haircut. All that was required now was an audition. Not easy for somebody with no acting experience.

Lazenby went to Eon offices in London. All he had to do was get past the receptionist downstairs. What sort of excuse could be used for that? Well none so the direct approach was taken… Crouch down behind the desk out of sight, shimmy along and then just bolt on up the stairs before anyone could say anything. And that is just what he did. As shouts from downstairs came, George continued running up those stairs. He burst into the room at the top and said "I heard you are looking for a new Bond?"

Harry Saltzman said "I have never heard of you, where have you acted?" Fearing he would fall at the first hurdle, George quickly made up a CV in his head, hoping Saltzman would be unable to verify it… "Germany, Czechoslovakia, Russia, couple of films in Hong Kong". Harry looked impressed. "Can you be here at 4 o'clock tomorrow?" he asked. George was suddenly filled with not only joy at getting an opportunity to test for Bond, but worry. Suddenly he knew he was well out of his depth.

The following day at 4pm, George Lazenby arrived for his audition in front of Director, Peter R. Hunt. Peter turned to him and asked "so what have you done?" In panic George turned to him and confessed to having never acted. For a moment Peter sat still. Suddenly he burst out laughing and said "you have fooled two of the most ruthless guys I have ever met to get here… You are an actor. Stick to your story and I'll make you the next James Bond".

Principle photography began in the Canton of Bern in Switzerland on the 21st of October, 1968, with the first scene shot being an aerial view of Bond climbing the stairs of Blofeld's mountain retreat to meet the girls. The scenes were shot atop the now famous revolving restaurant Piz Gloria, located atop the Schilthorn near the village of Mürren. The location was found by production manager Hubert Fröhlich after three weeks of location scouting in France and Switzerland. The restaurant was still under construction, but the producers found the location perfect, and had to finance providing electricity and the aerial lift to make filming there possible. Various chase scenes in the Alps were shot at Lauterbrunnen and Saas-Fee, while the Christmas celebrations were filmed in Grindelwald, and some scenes were shot on location in Bern. Production was hampered by weak snowfall which was unfavourable to the skiing action scenes. The Swiss filming ended up running 56 days over schedule. In March of 1969, production moved to Pinewood for interior shooting, and M's house being shot in Marlow, Buckinghamshire. In April, the filmmakers went to Portugal, where principal photography wrapped in May.

While the first unit shot at Piz Gloria, the second unit, led by John Glen, started filming the ski chases. The downhill skiing involved professional skiers, and various camera tricks. Some cameras were handheld, with the operators holding them as they were going downhill with the stuntmen, and others were aerial, with cameramen Johnny Jordan developing a system where he was dangled by an 18 feet (5.5 m) long parachute harness rig below a helicopter, allowing scenes to be shot on the move from any angle. The bobsledding chase was also filmed with the help of Swiss Olympic athletes, and was rewritten to incorporate the accidents the stuntmen suffered during shooting, such as the scene where Bond falls from the sled.

The avalanche scenes were due to be filmed in co-operation with the Swiss army who annually used explosions to prevent snow build-up by causing avalanches, but the area chosen naturally avalanched just before filming. The final result was a combination of a man-made avalanche at an isolated Swiss location shot by the second unit, stock footage, and images created by the special effects crew with salt. The stuntmen were filmed later, added by optical effects. For the scene where Bond and Tracy crash into a car race while being pursued, an ice rink was constructed over an unused aeroplane track, with water and snow sprayed on it constantly. Lazenby and Rigg did most of the driving due to the high number of close-ups.

Despite all the hard work, Lazenby was having the time of his life. He was Bond. A dream had come true and George found himself in the limelight. He could go to any nightclub anywhere in the world, money became easy and some clubs would even pay him to turn up. After filming George would have a private helicopter take him down to the local villages at night. He would return in the limousine which would wait for him right where the helicopter had dropped him off and every night he would return drunk and with a different girl, sometimes more than one. Life couldn't get much better than this for George Lazenby but the high life was starting to worry both Saltzman and Broccoli. At this same time, a man named Ronan O'Rahilly had stepped forward as Lazenby's new manager. O'Rahilly was an Irish Businessman and creator of the offshore radio station Radio Caroline. He was also something of a Hippy and very 'anti-establishment'. He convinced Lazenby that Broccoli and Saltzman were monsters and out to use him. O'Rahilly explained that the hippy movement was coming in and everything was about peace not war. There would be no future for James Bond in the 1970's amongst long hair and LSD. If George remained he would be typecast in the role and would go down with the sinking ship. With a seven movie deal in the pipeline for George to play Bond, he took O'Rahilly's advice. At the premiere for On Her Majesty's Secret Service, George grew his hair long and arrived with a big bushy beard. He looked more like he should have been in Easy Rider and was not the clean cut image of a James Bond. In the final hour, Saltzman and Broccoli withdrew the seven picture deal. They did not want to risk the future of Bond.

On Her Majesty's Secret Service was released on the 18th of December, 1969 with its premiere at the Odeon Leicester Square. The film topped the North American box office when it opened with a gross of $1.2 million. The film closed its box office run with £750,000 in the United Kingdom (the highest-grossing film of the year), $64.6 million worldwide, only half of You Only Live Twice's total gross, but still one of the highest-grossing films of 1969. It was one of the most popular movies in France in 1969, with admissions of 1,958,172. Nonetheless this was a considerable drop from the previous Bond movie.

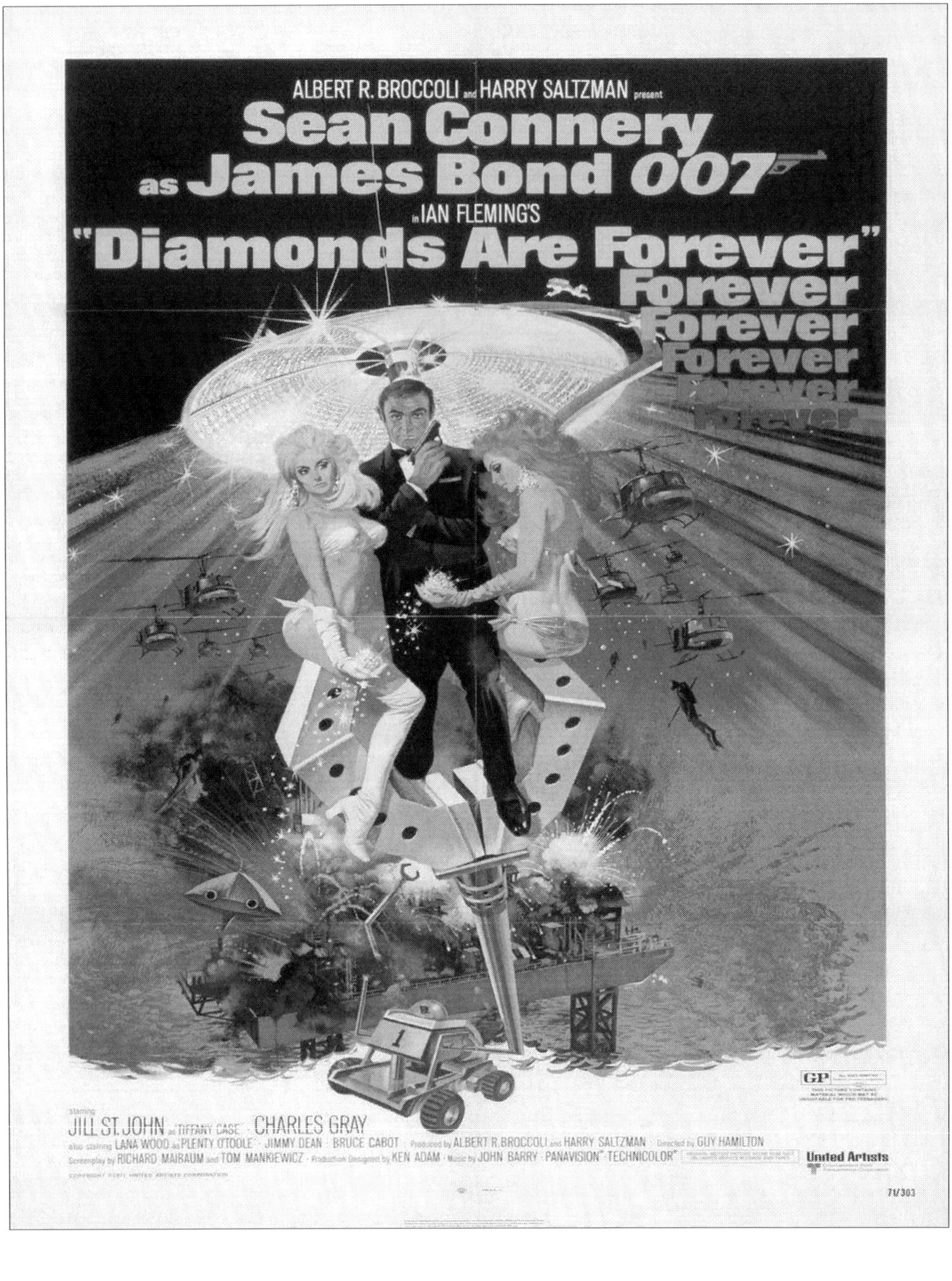
ALBERT R. BROCCOLI and HARRY SALTZMAN present
Sean Connery
as James Bond 007
in IAN FLEMING'S
"Diamonds Are Forever"
Forever
Forever
Forever
Forever
Forever
1
GP
starring
JILL ST. JOHN as "TIFFANY CASE" · CHARLES GRAY
also starring LANA WOOD as "PLENTY O'TOOLE" · JIMMY DEAN · BRUCE CABOT · Produced by ALBERT R. BROCCOLI and HARRY SALTZMAN · Directed by GUY HAMILTON
Screenplay by RICHARD MAIBAUM and TOM MANKIEWICZ · Production Designed by KEN ADAM · Music by JOHN BARRY · PANAVISION® · TECHNICOLOR®
United Artists
71/303

DIAMONDS ARE FOREVER

And so the search was on again for a new leading man. Producers contemplated John Gavin, Adam West (Batman) and even Michael Gambon. United Artists then stepped forward. They knew that to keep the Bond franchise alive they needed Connery back but that was not going to be easy. Connery certainly would not even consider the role if he were asked by Saltzman or Broccoli so United Artists offer him an unmissable deal. In return for portraying Bond again, Sean could have a two picture deal. Any two pictures he liked. It didn't matter what they were, if he wanted them he could have them and he would get a million dollars for each one plus $1.25 million to do the next Bond movie, Diamonds are Forever. Sean Connery would return…

Filming began on Diamonds are Forever on the 5th of April, 1971, with the South African scenes actually shot in the desert near Las Vegas. The film was shot primarily in the U.S., with locations including the L.A International Airport, Universal City Studios and various hotels around Las Vegas owned by Howard Hughes since he was a close friend of Cubby's. On return to filming in the U.K, production moved to Pinewood Studios as well as Dover and Southampton. The climactic oil rig sequence was shot off the shore of Oceanside, California and various other scenes were shot in Cap D'Antibes, France, Amsterdam and Lufthansa's hanger at Frankfurt Airport in Germany.

Getting the streets empty in order to shoot was achieved through the collaboration of Hughes, the Las Vegas police and shopkeepers association and the Las Vegas Hilton doubled for the Whyte House, and since the owner of the Circus Circus was a Bond fan, he allowed the Circus to be used on film and even made a cameo. The cinematographers said filming in Las Vegas at night had an advantage: no additional illumination was required due to the high number of neon lights. Sean Connery made the most of his time on location in Las Vegas. "I didn't get any sleep at all. We shot every night, I caught all the shows and played golf all day. On the weekend I collapsed…boy, did I collapse. Like a skull with legs." He also played the slot machines, and delayed one of the scenes because he was collecting his winnings.

The site used for the Willard Whyte Space Labs (where Bond gets away in the Moon Buggy) was actually, at that time, a Johns-Manville gypsum plant just outside of Las Vegas. The home of actor Kirk Douglas was used for the scene in Tiffany's house, while the Elrod House in Palm Springs became Willard Whyte's house. The exterior shots of the Slumber mortuary were of the Palm Mortuary in Henderson, Nevada. The interiors were on a set constructed back in the U.K. at

Pinewood Studios, where Ken Adam imitated the real building's lozenge-shaped stained glass window in its nave.

Since the car chase in Las Vegas would have many car crashes, the filmmakers had an arrangement with Ford to use their vehicles. Ford's only demand was that Sean Connery had to drive the 1971 Mustang Mach 1, which serves as Tiffany Case's car. The car chase where the red Mustang comes outside of the narrow street on the opposite side in which it was rolled, was filmed over three nights on Fremont Street in Las Vegas. The alleyway car roll sequence was actually filmed in two locations. The entrance was at the car park at Universal Studios and the exit was filmed by the second unit director at Fremont Street, Las Vegas. Because the two separate units filmed that scene in two separate locations is why the car goes in on its right side tyres and comes out on the left. By the time Hamilton had realised the mistake it was too late to shoot all over again so he put the actors in the car and filmed a brief few seconds showing the car sliding from one side to the next as a sort of explanation. It obviously did not work and audiences picked up on the mistake straight away. Not that anyone minded and the scene has since become one of the most recognised and remembered scenes of any Bond movie because of it.

While filming the scene of finding Plenty O'Toole drowned in Tiffany's swimming pool, Lana Wood actually had her feet loosely tied to a cement block on the bottom. Film crew members held a rope across the pool for her, with which she could lift her face out of the water to breathe between takes. The pool's sloping bottom made the block slip into deeper water with each take. Eventually, Wood was submerged but was noticed by on-lookers and rescued before actually drowning. Wood, being a certified diver, took some water but remained calm during the ordeal, although she later admitted to a few "very uncomfortable moments and quite some struggling until they pulled me out."

Diamonds are Forever was released on the 14th of December, 1971. The film grossed $116 million worldwide, of which $43 million was from audiences in the U.S.

HARRY SALTZMAN and ALBERT R. BROCCOLI present
ROGER MOORE as JAMES BOND
007
in IAN FLEMING'S
"LIVE AND LET DIE"
DEVIL
DEATH
LOVERS
FORTUNE
with
YAPHET KOTTO JANE SEYMOUR · Produced by HARRY SALTZMAN and ALBERT R. BROCCOLI · Directed by GUY HAMILTON
Screenplay by TOM MANKIEWICZ · Title Song Composed by PAUL and LINDA McCARTNEY and Sung by PAUL McCARTNEY and WINGS
Music Score by GEORGE MARTIN · COLOR
Original Motion Picture Soundtrack Available on United Artists Records and Tapes
MGM/UA
Entertainment Co

LIVE AND LET DIE

Connery declined another appearance as Bond, but the Producers already had another actor in mind. Roger Moore. Harry very much wanted Moore as the next Bond but Cubby had his doubts on whether Roger had the character for it. Roger Moore was more the charmer than tough guy. The two producers refused to agree over Moore and their relationship began to show strain as the two disagreed over the direction the character and the films should take. Harry had also become involved in a number of other businesses. Real Estate, Technicolor, and even a sausage factory were amongst Harry's new concentrations. Cubby began to feel that Harry was not showing enough interest in the Bond franchise. Harry had also been writing cheque's every which way and financial trouble was looming. Eventually the banks began calling in their debts. Harry had nowhere to turn and Cubby, worried over the future of Bond, offered to buy out Harry's share of the franchise but Harry refused to sell to him.

But the business continued for now. The two producers approached Clint Eastwood, who was fresh from his success as Dirty Harry. Eastwood turned down the offer, stating that 007 should be played by an Englishman. Among the actors to test for the part of Bond were Julian Glover, John Gavin, Jeremy Brett, William Gaunt and Michael Billington. The main frontrunner for the role was Michael Billington in the end but United Artists again wanted an American to play Bond. They suggested Burt Reynolds, Paul Newman, or Robert Redford. Saltzman kept pushing for Moore though and eventually Cubby backed down and Moore was offered the role.

With Roger Moore now the next James Bond planning for the next Bond adventure could get underway.

While filming Diamonds Are Forever, Live and Let Die had been chosen as the next Ian Fleming novel to be adapted because screenwriter Tom Mankiewicz thought it would be daring to use black villains, as the Black Panthers and other racial movements were active at this time. Guy Hamilton was again chosen to direct, and since he was a jazz fan, Mankiewicz suggested he film in New Orleans. Hamilton did not want to use Mardi Gras since Thunderball featured a similar festivity called the Junkanoo, so after more discussions with the writer and location scouting with helicopters, he decided to use two well-known features of the city; the jazz funerals and canals.

While searching for locations in Jamaica, the crew discovered a crocodile farm owned by a man named Ross Kananga, after passing a sign warning that "trespassers will be eaten." The farm was soon put into the script and the farm owner's name also inspired Mankiewicz to name the film's villain Kananga.

Mankiewicz had thought of turning Solitaire into a black woman, with Diana Ross as his primary choice but Broccoli and Saltzman decided to stick to Fleming's description of a white woman, and after considering Catherine Deneave, Jane Seymour was cast for the role. Yaphet Kotto was cast while doing another movie for United Artists called Across 110th Street.

To fit in with Moore's acting style, Mankiewicz added some comic relief to the scenes. In doing so he created Sheriff J.W. Pepper, portrayed by Clifton James.

Live and Let Die was the only Bond film up until 2006 not to feature Desmond Llewelyn's 'Q'. At the time, Llewelyn had been appearing in the TV series Follyfoot and the series producers had written him out of three episodes to allow him to film for Bond. Saltzman and Broccoli, however, decided not to include the character. They felt that "too much was being made of the films' gadgets", and decided to downplay this aspect of the series.

Principle photography began in October of 1972, in Louisiana. For a while only the second unit was shot after Moore had been diagnosed with kidney stones and needed to rest up. In November production moved to Jamaica, which doubled for the fictional San Monique and in December, production was divided between interiors in Pinewood Studios and location shooting in Harlem. After problems with a real life Harlem gang, and to ensure the crew's safety, filming was later moved to Manhattan's Upper East Side.

Ross Kananga, owner of the Crocodile farm, suggested the stunt where Bond jumps on crocodiles. The idea sounded great, "but only if you do it". And so Kananga was enlisted by the producers to perform it. The scene took five takes to be completed and very nearly went wrong on one take when the final crocodile opened its jaws just as Kananga jumped. Kananga's foot went into the crocodile's mouth and the tooth pierced his shoe. Kananga fell forwards and landed in the water but was able to pull his foot out of the now stuck shoe, and the crocodile's mouth, and pull himself up out of the water and to safety.

The production also had trouble with fear of snakes.

The script supervisor was so afraid that she refused to be on set with them, an actor fainted while filming a scene where he is killed by a snake, Jane Seymour became terrified as a reptile got closer, and Geoffrey Holder only agreed to fall into the snake-filled casket because Princess Alexandra was visiting the set.

The boat chase was filmed in Louisiana around the Irish Bayou area, with some interruption caused by flooding. Twenty-six boats were built by the Glastron boat company for the film. Seventeen of these were destroyed during rehearsals and the speedboat jump scene over the bayou, filmed with the assistance of a specially-constructed ramp, unintentionally set a Guinness World Record at the time with 110 feet (34 m) cleared. Unfortunately, the waves created by the impact caused the following boat to flip over.

Whilst filming in Jamaica, Guy Hamilton noticed that they used double-decker buses. Suddenly he thought... Bond in a Bus?

A second hand double-decker bus was promptly purchased and Roger Moore was taken to a skid pan to have a go. After a few days training, filming the bus chase began. Roger took to the wheel, but when it came to the famous driving under a low-bridge stunt somebody else had to take over. There were no stuntmen about at the time with experience with a double-decker bus so instead a real London bus driver was brought in. Maurice Patchett was a London Transport bus driving instructor and jumped at the opportunity. The bus was quickly adapted. Its top section was removed and then placed back on with a rail of ball bearings between the sections to allow the roof to naturally slide off and the bus was driven at the low bridge.

Live and Let Die was released in the United States on the 27th of June, 1973. The European premiere was again at Odeon Leicester Square in London on the 6th of July with general release in the United Kingdom on the same day. From a budget of around $7 million the film grossed $161.8 million and was a financial success. Even today the film holds the record for the most viewed broadcast film on television in the United Kingdom by attracting 23.5 million viewers when premiered on ITV back on the 20th of January, 1980.

EAST HEMI.

THE MAN WITH THE GOLDEN GUN

For the next Bond adventure a year later, Fleming's novel The Man with the Golden Gun was chosen. Filming commenced on the 6th of November, 1973, at the partly submerged wreck of the RMS Queen Elizabeth. The crew was small and initial shots of Moore playing Bond used a stunt double. Other Hong Kong locations included the Hong Kong Dragon Garden as the estate of Hai Fat, which portrayed a location in Bangkok. The major part of principle photography started on the 18th of April, 1974, in Thailand. Thai locations included Bangkok, Thon Buri, Phuket and the nearby Phang Nga Province, on the islands of Ko Khao Phing Kan and Ko Tapu. The scene during the boxing match used an actual Muay Thai fixture at the Lumpinee Boxing Stadium. In late April, production returned to Hong Kong, and later Macau for the casino scenes, as Hong Kong did not have Casinos. Scaramanga's solar energy plant and island interior were later shot at Pinewood.

Originally, the role of Scaramanga was offered to Jack Palance, but he turned the role down. Christopher Lee was eventually chosen to portray Scaramanga. Lee was Ian Fleming's step-cousin and Fleming had suggested Lee for the role of Dr. No back in 1962. Lee noted that Fleming was a forgetful man and by the time he mentioned this to Broccoli and Saltzman they had already cast Joseph Wiseman in the part.

Two Swedish models were cast as the Bond girls, Britt Ekland and Maud Adams. Ekland had been interested in playing a Bond girl since she had seen Dr. No, and contacted the producers about the main role of Mary Goodnight. Hamilton met Adams in New York, and cast her because "she was so elegant and beautiful that it seemed to me she was the perfect Bond girl". When Ekland read the news that Adams had been cast for The Man with the Golden Gun, she became upset, thinking Adams had been selected to play Goodnight. Broccoli then called Ekland to invite her for the main role, as after seeing her in a film, Broccoli thought Ekland's "generous looks" made her a good contrast to Adams. Hamilton decided to put Marc Lawrence, whom he had worked with on Diamonds Are Forever, to play a gangster shot dead by Scaramanga at the start of the film, because he found it an interesting idea to "put sort of a Chicago gangster in the middle of Thailand".

One of the main stunts in the film involved driving an AMC Hornet, leaping a broken bridge and spinning around 360 degrees in mid-air about the longitudinal axis in a cork screw effect. Before this stunt the little Hornet's only claim to fame was that it came with optional denim seat covers. Eon Productions had licensed the stunt, which had been designed by Raymond McHenry, years before and had been saving it for the right moment. The stunt was initially conceived at Cornell University Laboratory (CAL) in Buffalo, New York as a test for their powerful vehicle simulation software. This spiral jump was to be the most challenging Bond stunt yet and was the first movie stunt ever to use computers to work out all the details of the stunt. The AMC Hornet was carefully adapted including moving the steering wheel and driver's seat to the centre of the car so as to give it a perfect weight balance. Everything was ready, but the day of the planned jump the stunt man that had planned to do the stunt had to rush back to the U.S. for a family emergency. The cars mechanic, "Bumps" Willard, came forward and said "I'll do it". And he did it in one take. Cubby Broccoli was so impressed that as Bumps climbed out of the car, he ran over and placed a roll of $100 bills into Bumps hand. Bumps said "Can I do it again?"

The excitement was not over just yet though as Scaramanga makes his escape in dramatic fashion attaching wings to his AMC Matador and flying away (anybody would think AMC had sponsored the film to have their cars in it).

The AVE Mizar had originally been intended for use in The Man with the Golden Gun. It was a roadable aircraft built between 1971 and 1973 by Advanced Vehicle Engineers (AVE) of California. The Mizar was built by mating the rear of a Cesna Light Aircraft to a Ford Pinto. Perfect and just what was needed for the scene to work, and AVE were keen to lend the vehicle. However, shortly before filming the vehicles designer, Henry Smolinski and a second pilot, were up on a routine flight when the car body detached from the plane part. The car fell to the ground killing both drivers/pilots instantly. Eon were not so keen to use a real car after that and so two radio controlled models were constructed and used instead.

The Man with the Golden Gun was premiered at the Odeon Leicester Square in London on the 19th of December 1974, with general release in the United Kingdom the same day. The film was made with an estimated budget of $7 million. Despite initial good returns from the box office, The Man with the Golden Gun grossed a total of just $97.6 million at the worldwide box office, with $21 million earned in the USA, making it not quite the success all had hoped for.

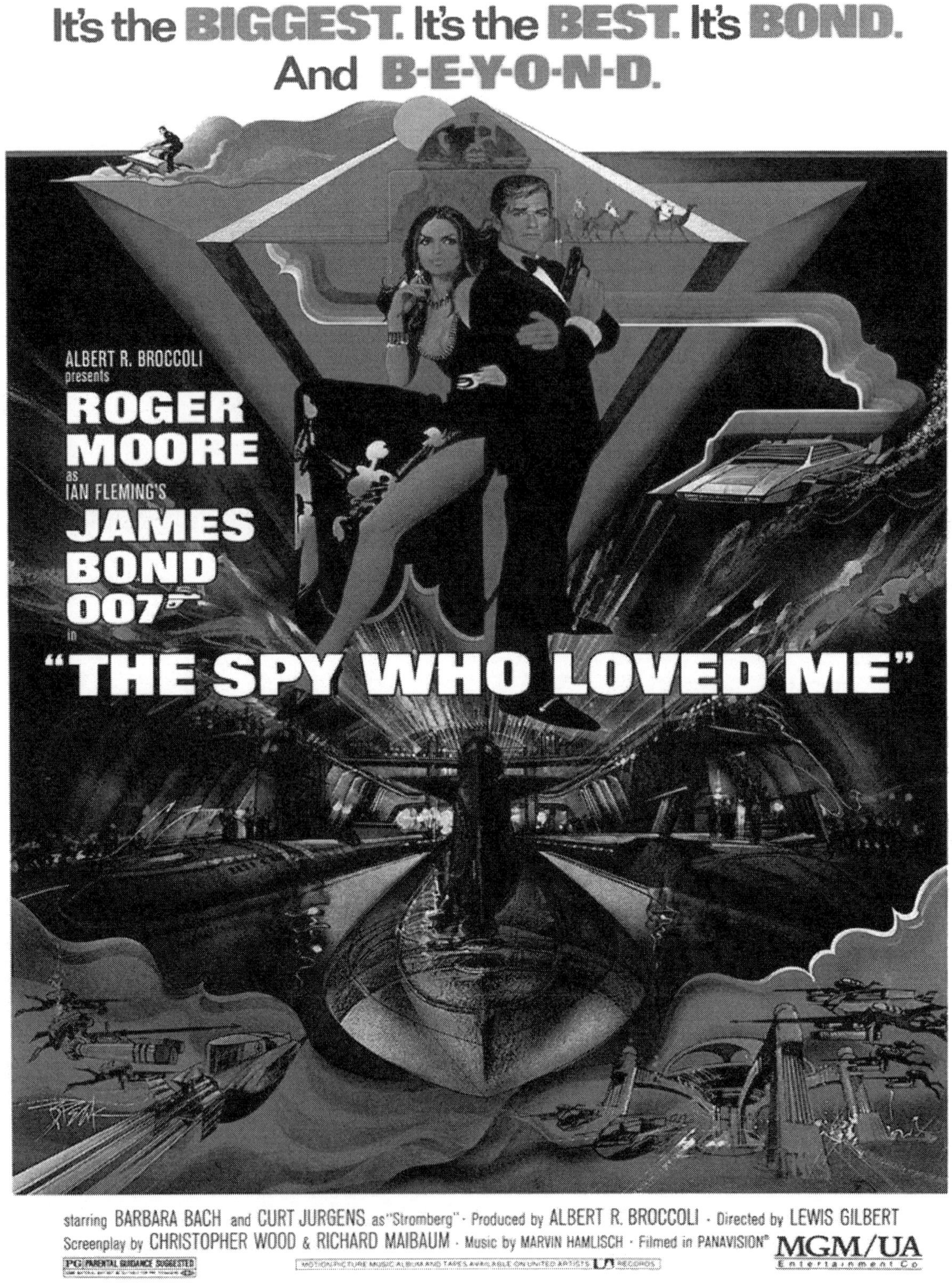

It's the BIGGEST. It's the BEST. It's BOND.
And B-E-Y-O-N-D.
ALBERT R. BROCCOLI
presents
ROGER
MOORE
as
IAN FLEMING'S
JAMES
BOND
007
in
"THE SPY WHO LOVED ME"
starring BARBARA BACH and CURT JURGENS as "Stromberg" · Produced by ALBERT R. BROCCOLI · Directed by LEWIS GILBERT
Screenplay by CHRISTOPHER WOOD & RICHARD MAIBAUM · Music by MARVIN HAMLISCH · Filmed in PANAVISION®
PG PARENTAL GUIDANCE SUGGESTED
MGM/UA
Entertainment Co

THE SPY WHO LOVED ME

Going back to 1969, Saltzman had borrowed 70 million Swiss Francs (US$40,000,000) from the Union Bank of Switzerland. The following year, in 1970, Saltzman had won control of the Technicolor Motion Picture Corporation from Chairman Patrick Frawley in a proxy fight, however by 1972 Saltzman had had to sell off 370,000 shares of Technicolor stock to repay his loan from the Union Bank of Switzerland. As he sold more shares the stock value dropped and Technicolor, for fear of going bust, had to take legal action to remove Saltzman from the board.

Saltzman's 1970s productions also proved problematic. A science fiction musical Tomorrow starring Olivia Newton-John was withdrawn from release and resulted in several lawsuits. Also in 1970 Saltzman cancelled a planned film several weeks before shooting was to begin about the dancer Vaslav Nijinsky starring Rudolf Nureyev. Director Tony Richardson believed that Saltzman had overextended himself and did not have the funds to make the film.

Eventually with Bankruptcy looming Harry had no choice but to sell his shares. But, instead of selling to Cubby he sold to United Artists. Suddenly Cubby had the studios as his partner in the franchise.

Harry Saltzman signed over to the studio at 4 o'clock in the morning for just $20,000,000. There was no celebration. A large portion of Harry's life had practically been given away. Financial doom still loomed and the Saltzman family had to sell everything. Personal possessions were gone and to make matters worse, Jacqueline Saltzman, Harry's wife, was diagnosed with terminal cancer.

Cubby knew that he would have to continue with Bond no matter what. The recent release of The Man with the Golden Gun had not been a huge success. Audience numbers had dramatically declined and in terms of James Bond, the film had been not far off of a failure. If the next film could only reach the same numbers then it could spell the end of Bond for good.

The Spy Who Loved Me was a huge gamble. The fate of Bond lay with the success of the film. Cubby put everything he had into it, double or nothing. It had to be the best Bond film yet and if it failed the money and the reputation would all be gone.

Before anything could start Cubby had to find a director. He approached Steven Spielberg, who was in post-production of Jaws, but ultimately decided to wait to see "how the fish picture turns out". Guy Hamilton was also offered the job but he declined after being offered the opportunity to direct the first Superman film although Richard Donner eventually done that instead. Eon Productions would later turn to Lewis Gilbert, who had directed You Only Live Twice.

With a director finally secured, the next hurdle was finishing the script, which had gone through several revisions by numerous writers. The initial villain of the film was Ernst Stavro Blofeld, however Kevin McClory, who owned the film rights to Thunderball forced an injunction on Eon Productions against using the character of Blofeld, or his international criminal organisation,

SPECTRE, which delayed production of the film further. The villain would later be changed from Blofeld to Stromberg so that the injunction would not interfere with the production. Christopher Wood was later brought in by Lewis Gilbert to complete the script. Although Fleming had originally requested that no elements from his original book are used if a film was made, the novel features two thugs named Sol Horror and Sluggsy Morent. Horror is described as having steel-capped teeth, while Sluggsy had a clear bald head. These characters would be the basis for the characters of Jaws and Sandor. Since Ian Fleming had permitted Eon to use only the name of his novel and not the actual novel, Fleming's name was moved for the first time from above the film's title to above "James Bond 007".

Broccoli commissioned a number of writers to work on the script, including Stirling Silliphant, John Landis, Ronald Hardy, Anthony Burgess, and Derek Marlowe. Eventually, Richard Maibaum provided the screenplay, and at first he tried to incorporate ideas from all of the other writers into his script. Maibaum's original script featured an alliance of international terrorists attacking SPECTRE's headquarters and disposing Blofeld, before trying to destroy the world for themselves to make way for a New World Order. However, this was soon shelved.

In the film, Stromberg's scheme to destroy civilisation by capturing Soviet and British nuclear submarines and have them fire intercontinental ballistic missiles at two major cities is actually a recycled plot from a previous Bond film, You Only Live Twice, which involved stealing space capsules to start a war between the Soviets and the Americans. The similarity was apparent in the climax and both films involved an assault on a heavily fortified enemy that had taken refuge behind steel shutters.

The film was shot at Pinewood Studios, Porto Cervo in Sardinia (Hotel Cala di Volpe), Egypt, Malta, Scotland, Hayling Island in the U.K., Okinawa, Switzerland and Mount Asgard on Baffin Island in the then northern Canadian Northwest Territories.

As no studio was big enough for the interior of Stromberg's super tanker, and set designer Ken Adam's did not want to repeat what he had done with SPECTRE's volcano base in You Only Live Twice, "a workable but ultimately wasteful set", construction began in March 1976 of a new sound stage at Pinewood, the 007 Stage. At a cost of $1.8 million the stage would also feature a water tank capable of storing approximately 1,200,000 gallons (4,500,000 litres). The soundstage was so huge that Stanley Kubrick visited the production, in secret, to advice on how to light the stage. For the exterior, while Shell was willing to lend an abandoned tanker to the production, the elevated insurance and safety risks caused it to be replaced with miniatures built by Derek Medding's team and shot in the Bahamas. Stromberg's shark tank was also filmed in the Bahamas, using a live shark in a saltwater swimming pool. Adam's decided to do experiments with curved shapes for the scenery, as he felt all his previous set pieces were "too linear". This was demonstrated with the Atlantis, which is a dome and curved surfaces outside, and many curved objects in Stromberg's office inside.

Don McLaughlan, then head of public relations at Lotus Cars, heard that Eon was shopping for a new Bond car. He naturally enough wanted it to be a Lotus. Don decided that rather than struggle to prove his cars to the Bond producers, along with every other car manufacturer, he would get them come looking for him. He drove a prototype Lotus Esprit with all Lotus branding taped over, and parked it outside the Eon offices at Pinewood studios. Sure enough the Bond bigwigs noticed the car. On seeing them all crowded around looking the car over he walked over, and without speaking to anyone, climbed in the car and drove off. He had gambled that they would remember and come looking for him. It worked and the Lotus Esprit became Bond's car for The Spy Who Loved Me. Don's 007 sized cajoneys had paid off.

In October, the second unit travelled to Nassau to film the underwater sequences. For the Lotus to become a submarine, some of the shots were filmed using the empty shell of an Esprit with two divers inside and the other bits were filmed using models. The car seen entering the sea was a mock-up shell, propelled off the jetty by a compressed air cannon. During the model sequences, the air bubbles seen appearing from the vehicle was created by Alka-Seltzer tablets.

In September, production moved to Egypt. While the Great Sphinx of Giza was shot on the location, lighting problems caused the Pyramids to be replaced with miniatures. The production team returned briefly to the UK to shoot at the Faslane submarine base before setting off to Spain,

Portugal and the Bay of Biscay where the super tanker exteriors were filmed. On the 5th of December, with principal photography finished, the 007 Stage was formally opened by former Prime Minister Harold Wilson.

It all worked. The opening night in Leicester Square on the 7th of July, 1977… an audience comprising of Princess Anne and the Prince of Wales sat down to watch the latest introduction to Bond. "But Bond I need you" said the blond girl. "So does England" replies Roger Moore. He turns, closes the cabin door and after a brief race to escape the baddies, ski's off of the edge of a mountain… the parachute opens revealing the Union Jack flag and the Bond theme begins. The audience went wild and even Prince Charles stood up. At that point and with that one scene, James Bond had gone from character to national treasure.

The film grossed $185.4 million worldwide, with $46 million in the United States alone.

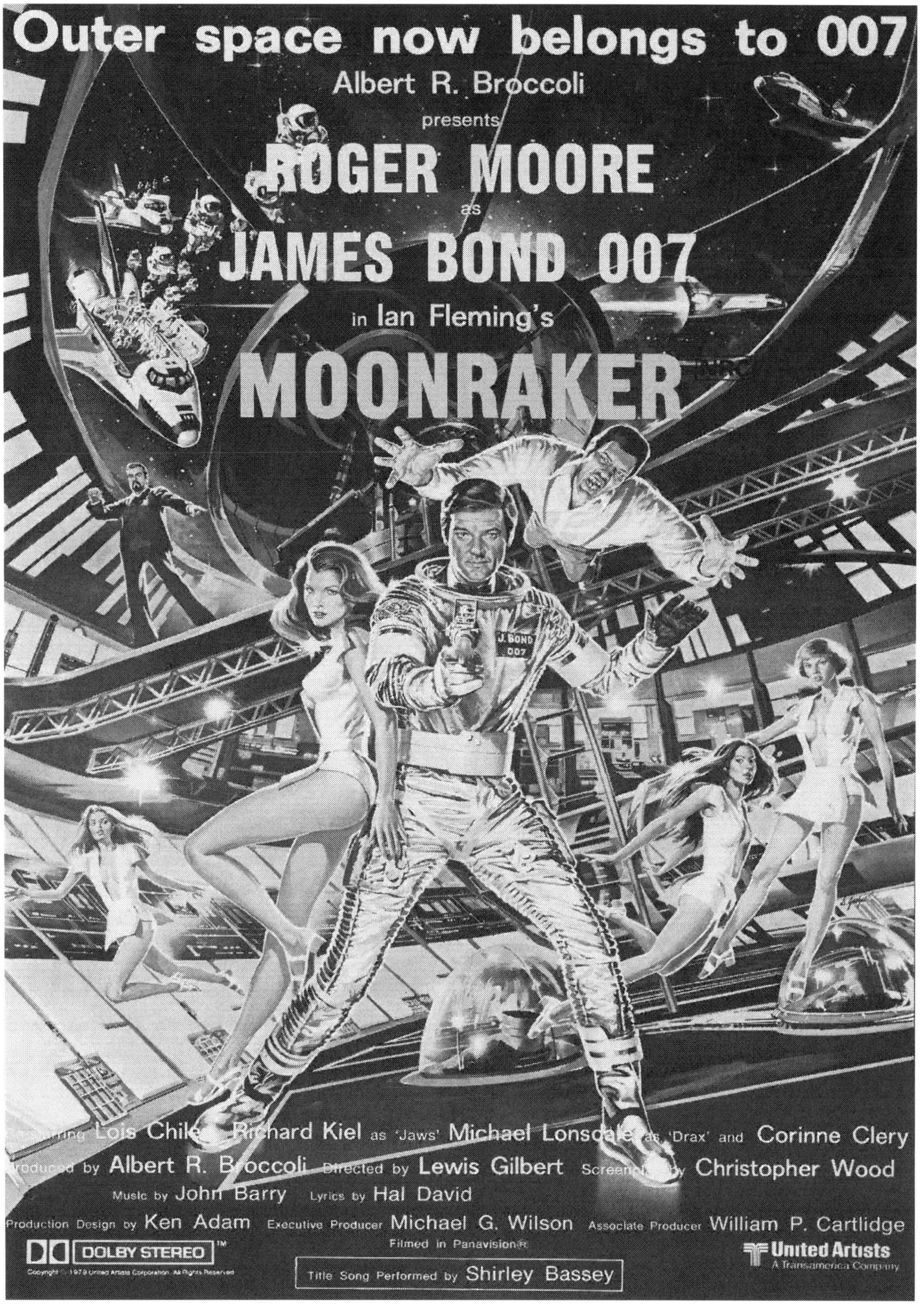

Outer space now belongs to 007
Albert R. Broccoli
presents
ROGER MOORE
as
JAMES BOND 007
in Ian Fleming's
MOONRAKER
J. BOND
007
Richard Kiel as 'Jaws' Michael Lonsdale as 'Drax' and Corinne Clery
by Albert R. Broccoli Directed by Lewis Gilbert Christopher Wood
Music by John Barry Lyrics by Hal David
Production Design by Ken Adam Executive Producer Michael G. Wilson Associate Producer William P. Cartlidge
Filmed in Panavision®
DOLBY STEREO™
Title Song Performed by Shirley Bassey
United Artists
A Transamerica Company

MOONRAKER

The end credits of The Spy Who Loved Me had read "James Bond will return in For Your Eyes Only" but, with the recent release and box office success of Star Wars, it was decided the next Bond film should be based upon Fleming's novel "Moonraker".

Moonraker had been written by Fleming, back in 1955, as a manuscript for a screenplay. American actor John Payne offered $1,000 for a nine month option to Moonraker, plus $10,000 if production eventually took off. The negotiations broke up the following year due to disagreements regarding Payne's ownership of the other Bond novels and so Fleming eventually settled with Rank Organisation, a British company who owned Pinewood Studios. Rank wound up not developing the film, even after Fleming contributed his own script trying to push production forward, and Fleming purchased the rights back in 1959. He then re-wrote Moonraker as a novel. It was to become the last James Bond novel to get a screen adaptation.

However, as with several previous Bond films, the story from Fleming's novel is almost entirely dispensed with, and little more than the name of Hugo Drax was used in film, in favour of a film more in keeping with the era of science fiction.

Tom Mankiewicz wrote a short outline for Moonraker that was mostly discarded. Footage shot at Drax's lairs was considerably more detailed than the edited result in the final version of the film. The crew had shot a scene with Drax meeting his co-financiers in his jungle lair and they used the same chamber room below the space shuttle launch pad that Bond and Goodhead eventually escape from. This scene was shot but later cut out. Another scene involving Bond and Goodhead in a meditation room aboard Drax's space station was shot but never used in the final film. However, press stills were released of the scene which featured on Topps trading cards in 1979 as was a cinema trailer which featured a close-up of Jaws reaction after Bond punches him in the face aboard the space station, neither of which featured in the complete film. Some scenes from Mankiewicz's script were later used in subsequent films, including the Acrostar Jet sequence used in the pre-credit sequence for Octopussy, and the Eiffel Tower scene in A View to a Kill.

The screenplay of Moonraker differed so much from Ian Fleming's novel that Eon Productions authorised the film's screenwriter, Christopher Wood to write a novelization. It was named James Bond and Moonraker to avoid confusion with Fleming's original novel and was published in 1979 coinciding with the film's release.

Initially, the chief villain, Hugo Drax, was to be played by British actor James Mason, but once the decision was made that the film would be an Anglo-French co-production under the 1965–79 film treaty, French actor Michael Lonsdale was cast as Drax and Corinne Cléry was chosen for the part of Corinne Dufour, in order to comply with qualifying criteria of the agreement. American actress Lois Chiles had originally been offered the role of Anya Amasova in The Spy Who Loved Me (1977), but had turned down the part when she decided to take temporary retirement. Chiles was cast as Holly Goodhead by chance, when she was given the seat next to Lewis Gilbert on a flight and he believed she would be ideal for the role as the CIA scientist. Drax's henchman Chang, played by Japanese aikido instructor Toshiro Suga, was recommended for the role by Michael Wilson, who was one of his pupils. In Moonraker, Wilson also continued a tradition in the Bond films he started in the film Goldfinger where he has a small cameo role. He appears twice in the film, first as a tourist outside the Venini Glass shop and museum in Venice, then at the end of the film as a technician in Drax's control room.

The Jaws character, played by Richard Kiel made a return, although in Moonraker the role is played more for comedic effect than in The Spy Who Loved Me. Jaws was intended to be a villain against Bond to the bitter end, but he received so much fan mail from small children saying "Why can't Jaws be a goodie not a baddie", that as a result he was persuaded to make Jaws gradually become Bond's ally at the end of the film.

Diminutive French actress Blanche Ravalec, who had only recently begun her career with minor roles in French films such as Michel Lang's Holiday Hotel (1978) and Claude Sautet's A Simple Story (1978), was cast as the bespectacled Dolly, the girlfriend of Jaws. Originally, the producers were dubious about whether the audience would accept the height difference between them, and only made their decision once they were informed by Richard Kiel that his real-life wife was of the same height. Lois Maxwell's (Moneypenny) 22-year old daughter, Melinda Maxwell, was also cast as one of the "perfect" human specimens from Drax's master race.

Production of Moonraker began on the 14th of August, 1978. The main shooting was switched from the usual 007 Stage at Pinewood to France, due to high taxation in England at the time. Only the cable car interiors and space battle exteriors were filmed at Pinewood. The massive sets designed by Ken Adam were the largest ever constructed in France and required more than 222,000 man-hours to construct (roughly 1000 hours by each of the crew on average). They were shot at three of France's largest film studios in Epinay and Boulogne-Billancourt. 220 technicians used 100 tonnes of metal, two tonnes of nails and 10,000 feet of wood to build the three-story space station set at Eponay Studios. The elaborate space set for Moonraker holds the world record for having the largest number of zero gravity wires in one scene. The Venetian glass museum and fight between Bond and Chang was shot at Boulogne Studios in a building which had once been a Luftwaffe aircraft factory during Germany's occupation of France. The scene in the Venice glass museum and warehouse holds the record for the largest amount of break-away Sugar-glass used in a single scene

Drax's mansion, set in California, was actually filmed at the Chateau de Vaux-le-Vicomte, about 55 kilometres (34 mi) southeast of Paris, for the exteriors and Grand Salon. The remaining interiors, including some of the scenes with Corinne Defour and the drawing room, were filmed at the Chateau de Guermantes.

Much of the film was shot in London, Paris, Venice, California, Florida, and Rio de Janeiro. The production team had considered India and Nepal as a location in the film but on arriving at those places to investigate, they found that it was inconceivable to write them into the script, particularly with time restrictions to do so. They decided on Rio de Janeiro, Brazil, relatively early on, a city that Cubby Broccoli had visited on holiday, and a team was sent to that city in early 1978 to capture initial footage from the Carnaval festival, which later featured in the film

At the Rio de Janeiro location, many months later, Roger Moore arrived several days later than scheduled for shooting due to recurrent health problems and an attack of kidney stones that he had suffered while in France. After arriving in Rio de Janeiro, Moore was immediately whisked off the plane and went straight to hair and make-up work, before re-boarding the plane, to film the sequence with him arriving as James Bond in the film. Sugarloaf Mountain was a prominent location in the film, and during filming of the cable car sequence in which Bond and Goodhead are attacked by Jaws during mid-air transportation high above Rio de Janeiro, the stuntman Richard Graydon slipped and narrowly avoided falling to his death. For the scene in which Jaws bites into the steel tramway cable with his teeth, the cable was actually made of liquorice, although Richard Kiel was still required to use his steel dentures.

Iguazu Falls was a natural location depicted in the film, although as stated by "Q" in the film, the falls were intended to be located somewhere in the upper basin of the Amazon River rather than where the falls are actually located in the south of Brazil. The second unit had originally planned on sending an actual boat over the falls, however on attempting to release it, the boat became firmly embedded on rocks near the edge. Despite a dangerous attempt by helicopter and rope ladder to retrieve it, the plan had to be abandoned, forcing the second unit to use a miniature at Pinewood instead. The exterior of Drax's pyramid headquarters in the Amazon rain forest near the falls was actually filmed at the Tikal Mayan ruins in Guatemala. The interior of the pyramid, however, was designed by Ken Adam at a French studio, in which he purposefully used a shiny coating to make the walls look plastic and false. All of the space centre scenes were shot at the Vehicle Assembly Building of the Kennedy Space Centre in Florida and the Rockwell International manufacturing plant in Palmdale, California.

The early scene involving Bond and Jaws in which Bond is pushed out of the aircraft without a parachute took weeks of planning and preparation. The skydiving sequence was coordinated by Don Calvedt under the supervision of second unit director John Glen. As Calvedt and skydiving champion B.J. Worth developed the equipment for the scene, which included a 1-inch-thick (25 mm) parachute pack that could be concealed beneath the suit to give the impression of the missing parachute, and equipment to prevent the freefalling cameraman from suffering whiplash while opening his parachute, they brought in stuntman Jake Lombard to test it all. Lombard eventually played Bond in the scene, with Worth as the pilot from which Bond takes a parachute, and Ron Luginbill as Jaws. Both Lombard and Worth would become regular members of the stunt team for aerial sequences in later Bond films. When the stuntmen opened their parachutes at the end of every shoot, custom-sewn Velcro costume seams would separate to allow the hidden parachutes to open. The skydiver cinematographer used a lightweight Panavision camera, bought from an old pawn shop in Paris, which he had adapted, and attached to his helmet to shoot the entire sequence. The scene took a total of 88 skydives by the stuntmen to be completed. The only scenes shot in studio were close-ups of Roger Moore and Richard Kiel.

For the scene involving the opening of the musical electronic laboratory door lock in Venice, Cubby. Broccoli requested special permission from director Steven Spielberg to use the five-note melody from his film Close Encounters' of the Third Kind (1977). In 1985, Broccoli would return the favour by fulfilling Spielberg's request to use the James Bond theme music for a scene in his film, The Goonies (1985).

Moonraker premiered on June the 26th, 1979, in the United Kingdom, grossing $70,308,099. Three days after the U.K. release, it went on general release in the U.S, opening in 788 cinemas. In Europe, Moonraker opened in August in the Scandinavian countries of Denmark, Finland, Norway, and Sweden between the 13th and 18th of August. Given that the film was produced largely in France, and it involved some notable French actors, the French premiere for the film was relatively late, released in that country on the 10th of October. Moonraker grossed a worldwide total of $210,300,000.

No one comes close to JAMES BOND 007

ALBERT R. BROCCOLI presents
ROGER MOORE
as IAN FLEMING'S
JAMES BOND 007
in
FOR YOUR EYES ONLY

Starring CAROLE BOUQUET • TOPOL • LYNN-HOLLY JOHNSON • JULIAN GLOVER
Produced by ALBERT R. BROCCOLI • Directed by JOHN GLEN
Screenplay by RICHARD MAIBAUM and MICHAEL G. WILSON • Executive Producer MICHAEL G. WILSON
Music by BILL CONTI • Production Designer PETER LAMONT
Associate Producer TOM PEVSNER

United Artists

Title Song Performed by SHEENA EASTON

FOR YOUR EYES ONLY

For Your Eyes Only marked a change in the make-up of the production crew. Film Editor John Glen was promoted to Director, a position he would occupy for another four films. The transition in directors resulted in a harder-edged directorial style, with less emphasis on gadgetry and large action sequences in huge arenas. Emphasis was placed on tension, plot and character in addition to a return to Bond's more serious roots, whilst For Your Eyes Only "showed a clear attempt to activate some lapsed and inactive parts of the Bond mythology."

The film was also a deliberate effort to bring the series more back to reality, following the huge excess of Moonraker in 1979. To that end, the story that emerged was simpler, not one in which the world was at risk, but returning the series to that of a Cold War thriller. Bond would also rely more on his wits than gadgets to survive. Glen decided to symbolically represent it with a scene where Bond's Lotus blows itself up and forces 007 to rely on Melina's more humble Citroën 2CV. Since Ken Adam's was busy with the film Pennies from Heaven, Peter Lamont, who had worked in the art department since Goldfinger, was promoted to production designer. Following a suggestion of Glen's, Lamont created realistic scenery, instead of the elaborate set pieces for which the series had been known.

Richard Maibaum was once again the scriptwriter for the story, assisted by Michael G. Wilson. According to Wilson, the ideas from stories could have come from anyone as the outlines were worked out in committee that could include Broccoli, Maibaum, Wilson and various stunt coordinators. Much of the inspiration for the stories for the film came from two Ian Fleming short stories from the collection For Your Eyes Only: "Risico" and "For Your Eyes Only". Another set-piece from the novel of Live and Let Die, the keelhauling, which was unused in the film of the same name, was also inserted into the plot. Other ideas from Fleming were also used in For Your Eyes Only, such as the Identigraph, which come from the novel Goldfinger, where it was originally called the "Identicast". These elements from Fleming's stories were mixed with a Cold War story.

The beginning sequence of the film shows Bond laying flowers at the grave of his wife, Tracy Bond, before a Universal Exports helicopter picks him up for an emergency. Control of the helicopter is taken over by remote control by a bald man in a grey jacket with a white cat. This character is unnamed in either the film or the credits, although he looks and sounds like Ernst Stavro Blofeld. Director John Glen later referred to the identity of the villain obliquely: "We just let people use their imaginations and draw their own conclusions ... It's a legal thing". The character is deliberately not named due to copyright restrictions with Kevin McClory owning the rights to Blofeld and SPECTRE. The helicopter scenes were filmed at the abandoned Beckton Gas Works in London. The gas works were also the location for Stanley Kubrick's 1987 film, Full Metal Jacket.

Bernard Lee died in January of 1981, after filming had started on For Your Eyes Only, but before he could film his scenes as M. Out of respect, no new actor was hired to assume the role and, instead, the script was re-written so that the character is said to be on leave, letting Chief of Staff Bill Tanner take over the role as acting head of MI6 and briefing Bond alongside the Minister of Defence. Chaim Topol was cast following a suggestion by Broccoli's wife Dana, while Julian Glover joined the cast as the producers felt he was stylish. Interestingly Glover was even considered to play Bond once before and had auditioned for the role but at the time he was considered too young. Carole Bouquet was a suggestion of United Artists publicist Jerry Juroe, and after Glen and Broccoli saw her in That Obscure Object of Desire, they went to Rome to invite Bouquet for the role of Melin

Production of For Your Eyes Only began on the 2nd of September, 1980 in the North Sea. Three days were spent shooting exterior scenes with the St Georges. The interiors were shot later at Pinewood, as well as the ship's explosion, which was done with a miniature on the 007 stage tank. On the 15th of September, principle photography started on Corfu at the Villa Sylva at Kanoni, above Corfu Town, which acted as the location of the Spanish villa. Many of the local houses were painted white for scenographic reasons. Glen opted to use the local slopes and olive trees for the chase scene between Melina's Citroën 2CV and Gonzales' men driving Peugeot 504's The scene was shot across twelve days, with stunt driver Remy Julienne driving the Citroën. Four 2CVs were used, with modifications for the stunts. All had more powerful flat-four engines, and one received a special revolving plate on its roof so it could get turned upside down.

In October filming moved to other Greek locations, including Metéora and the Achilleion. In November, the main unit moved to England, which included interior work in Pinewood, while the second unit shot underwater scenes in The Bahamas. On the 1st of January, 1981, production moved to Cortina D'Ampezzo in Italy, where filming wrapped in the February. Since it was not snowing in Cortina D'Ampezzo by the time of filming, the producers had to pay for trucks to bring snow from nearby mountains, which was then dumped in the city's streets.

Many of the underwater scenes, especially involving close-ups of Bond and Melina, were actually faked on a dry soundstage. A combination of lighting effects, slow-motion photography, wind, and bubbles added in post-production, gave the illusion of the actors being underwater. Actress Carole Bouquet reportedly had a pre-existing health condition that prevented her from performing actual underwater stunt work.

Roger Moore was reluctant to film the scene of Bond kicking a car, with Locque inside, over the edge of a cliff, saying that it "was Bond-like, but not Roger Moore Bond-like." Michael G. Wilson later said that Moore had to be persuaded to be more ruthless than he felt comfortable. Wilson also added that he and Richard Maibaum, along with John Glen, toyed with other ideas surrounding that scene, but ultimately everyone, even Moore, agreed to do the scene as originally written

For the Metéora shoots, a Greek bishop was paid to allow filming in the monasteries, but the uninformed Eastern Orthodox monks were mostly critical of production rolling in their installations. After a trial in the Greek Supreme Court, it was decided that the monks' only property were the interiors (the exteriors and surrounding landscapes belonged to the local government). In protest, the monks remained shut inside the monasteries during the shooting, and tried to sabotage production as much as possible, hanging their washing out of their windows and covering the principal monastery with plastic bunting and flags to spoil the shots, and placing oil drums to prevent the film crew from landing helicopters. The production team solved the problem with back lighting, matte paintings, and building both a similar scenographic monastery on a nearby unoccupied rock, and a monastery set in Pinewood.

Roger Moore said he had a great fear of heights, and to do the climbing in Greece, he resorted to moderate drinking to calm his nerves. Later in that same sequence, Rick Sylvester, a stuntman who had previously performed the pre-credits ski jump in The Spy Who Loved Me, undertook the stunt of Bond falling off the side of the cliff. The stunt was dangerous, since the sudden rope jerk at the bottom could be fatal. Special effects supervisor Derek Medding's developed a system that would dampen the stop, but Sylvester recalled that his nerves nearly got the better of him: "From where we were shooting, you could see the local cemetery; and the box to stop my fall looked like a casket. You didn't need to be an English major to connect the dots".

Bond veteran cameraman and professional skier Willy Bogner, Jr. was promoted to director of a second unit involving ski footage. Bogner designed the ski chase on the bobsleigh track of Cortina d'Ampezzo hoping to surpass his work in both On Her Majesty's Secret Service and The Spy Who Loved Me. To allow better filming, Bogner developed both a system where he was attached to a bobsleigh, allowing him to film the vehicle in front or behind it, and a set of skis that allowed him to ski forwards and backwards in order to get the best shots. In February of 1981, on the final day of filming the bobsleigh chase, one of the stuntmen driving the sleigh, 23-year-old Paolo Rigon, fell and became trapped under it. He was killed almost instantly.

For Your Eyes Only was premiered at the Odeon Leicester Square in London on the 24th of June, 1981. The film set an all-time opening-day record for any film at any cinema in the U.K. with a gross of £14,998. The film went on general release in the U.K. the same day. For Your Eyes Only had its North American premiere in the U.S. and Canada on Friday the 26th of June, at approximately 1,100 cinemas.

The film grossed $54.8 million in the United States and $195.3 million worldwide, becoming the second highest grossing Bond film after its predecessor, Moonraker. This was the last James Bond film to be solely released by United Artists as the following year they merged with MGM.

SEAN CONNERY

is JAMES BOND in

NEVER SAY NEVER AGAIN

JACK SCHWARTZMAN and KEVIN McCLORY Present
A TALIAFILM Production An IRVIN KERSHNER Film
SEAN CONNERY
"NEVER SAY NEVER AGAIN"
Also starring KLAUS MARIA BRANDAUER · MAX VON SYDOW · BARBARA CARRERA · KIM BASINGER
BERNIE CASEY · ALEC McCOWEN and EDWARD FOX as "M" Director of Photography DOUGLAS SLOCOMBE B.S.C.
Music by MICHEL LEGRAND Executive Producer KEVIN McCLORY Screenplay by LORENZO SEMPLE, JR.
Based on an Original Story by KEVIN McCLORY, JACK WHITTINGHAM and IAN FLEMING Directed by IRVIN KERSHNER
Produced by JACK SCHWARTZMAN Title song sung by LANI HALL Music by MICHEL LEGRAND Lyrics by ALAN and MARILYN BERGMAN

NEVER SAY NEVER AGAIN

With the Bond franchise back in full swing again came the re-emergence of an old problem. Kevin McClory had resurfaced. His ten year tenure on the Thunderball film had ended and, as his contract had allowed for, he was now free to do with Thunderball as he wished. Kevin wanted Bond for himself and now it seemed possible to do so. He approached Sean Connery and asked if he wanted to return as James Bond in an independent James Bond adventure and Sean agreed. Now McClory had a trump card. He could make Bond and had Connery as his leading man. A remake of Thunderball had huge potential and so the pair got together on making Never Say Never Again.

Cubby Broccoli could never have imagined that McClory would actually go ahead and try to remake Thunderball or he would never have agreed to that part of McClory's contract. Eon Productions were beginning work on Octopussy and McClory could put their efforts to vein. Octopussy had to be more successful than McClory's version. It simply had to be better. Now we had the battle of the Bond's.

Filming for Never Say Never Again had begun on the 27th of September, 1982, on the French Riviera. Two months later the crew moved to Nassau and filming started at Clifton Pier (Clifton Pier was also used for filming in Thunderball). The Spanish city of Almeria was also later used as a location. Largo's Palmyran fortress was actually historic Fort Carré in Antibes and for Largo's ship, the Flying Saucer, the yacht Nabila, owned by Saudi billionaire Adnan Khashoggi was used.

Production on the film was troubled, with Connery taking on many of the production duties with assistant director David Tomblin. Director Irvin Kershner was critical of producer Jack Schwartzman, saying that whilst he was a good businessman, "he didn't have the experience of a film producer". After the production ran out of money, Schwartzman had to fund further production out of his own pocket and later admitted he had underestimated the amount the film would cost to make.

The film underwent one final change in title before being released (it had originally gone by the names "Warhead" and "James Bond of the Secret Service"). After Connery had finished filming Diamonds Are Forever he had pledged that he would "never" play Bond again. Connery's wife, Micheline, suggested the title Never Say Never Again, referring to her husband's vow and the producers acknowledged her contribution by listing her on the end credits "Title "Never Say Never Again" by: Micheline Connery". A final attempt by Fleming's trustees to block the film was made in the High Courts in London in the spring of 1983, but these were thrown out by the court and Never Say Never Again was permitted to proceed.

For the main villain in the film, Maximillian Largo, Connery suggested Klaus Maria Brandauer, the lead of the 1981 Academy Award-winning Hungarian film Mephisto. Through the same route came Max von Sydow as Ernst Stavro Blofeld, although he still retained his Eon-originated white cat in the film. For the femme fatale, Director Irvin Kershner selected former model and Playboy cover girl Barbara Carrera to play Fatima Blush, the name coming from one of the early scripts of Thunderball Micheline Connery, Sean's wife, had met up-and-coming actress Kim Basinger at a hotel in London and suggested her to Connery, which he agreed upon. For the role of Felix Leiter, Connery spoke with Bernie Casey, saying that as the Leiter role was never remembered by audiences, using a black Leiter might make him more memorable. Others cast included comedian Rowan Atkinson, who would later parody Bond in his role of Johnny English.

Former Eon Productions' editor and director of On Her Majesty's Secret Service, Peter R. Hunt, was approached to direct the film but declined due to his previous work with Eon. Irvin Kershner, who had achieved success in 1980 with The Empire Strikes Back was then hired. A number of the crew from the 1981 film Raiders of the Lost Ark were also appointed. Many of the elements of the Eon-produced Bond films were not present in Never Say Never Again for legal reasons. These included the gun barrel sequence, where a screen full of 007 symbols appeared instead, and similarly there was no "James Bond Theme" to use, although no effort was made to supplement another tune. Never Say Never Again did not use a pre-credits sequence. One was filmed but later discarded. Instead the film opens with the credits run over the top of the opening sequence of Bond on a training mission. Another difference from EON films was the character of Q. As Q was a copyright character of Fleming and EON films, he could not be used in this film. Accordingly, the character in this film who serves exactly the same function as Q (providing gadgets) is named Algy, so as to avoid copyright infringements.

Principal photography finished at Elstree Studios where interior shots were filmed.

The two films were released almost simultaneously. Viewing figures were watched more closely than they had ever been before. Both Cubby and McClory wanted the highest numbers. For Cubby it paid off. Never Say Never Again, although still a profitable film, could not quite match the audience numbers of Octopussy. It proved that James Bond could not be made successful with only one ingredient in the recipe. Simply having Sean Connery was not enough.

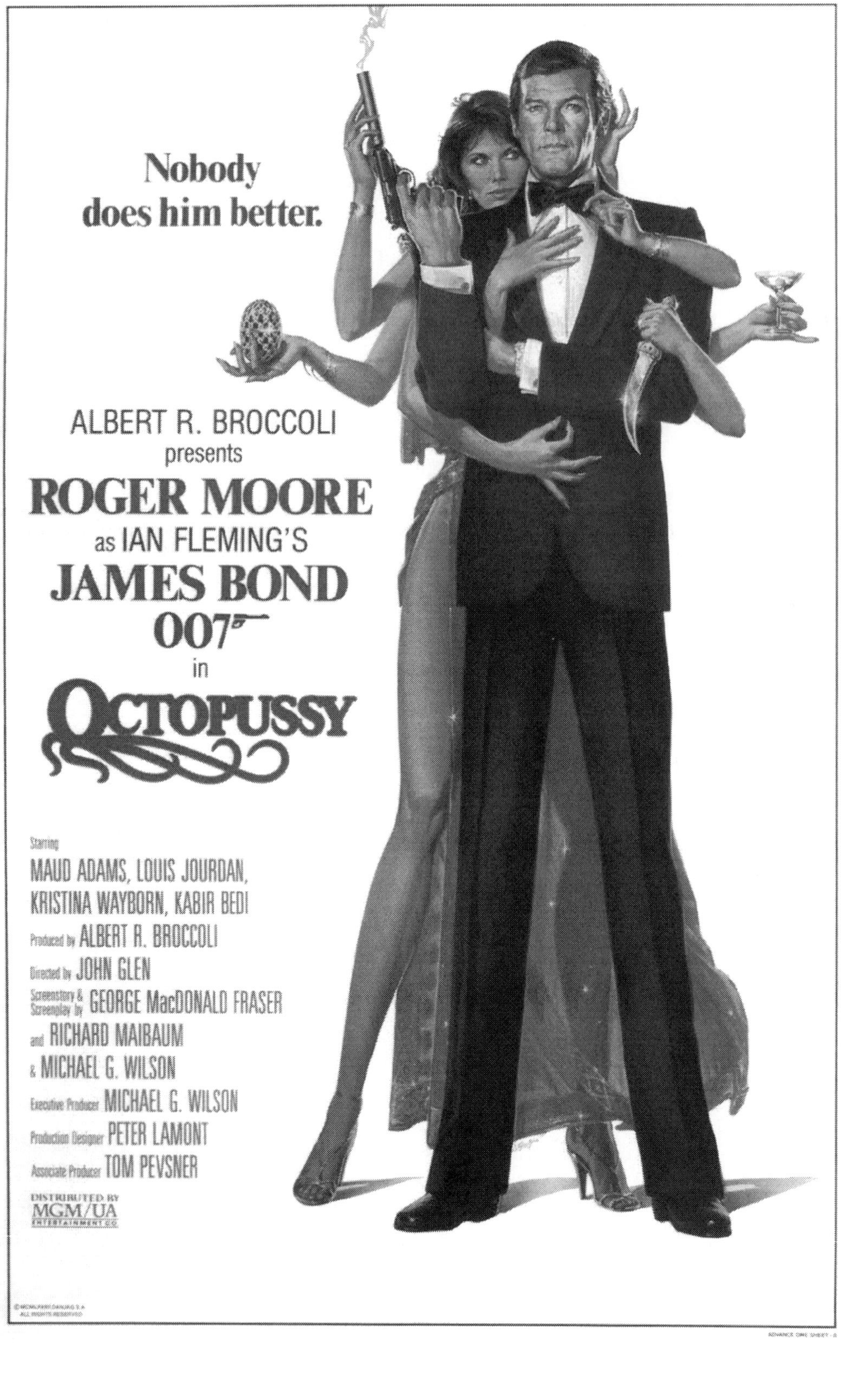

Nobody
does him better.
ALBERT R. BROCCOLI
presents
ROGER MOORE
as IAN FLEMING'S
JAMES BOND
007
in
OCTOPUSSY
Starring
MAUD ADAMS, LOUIS JOURDAN,
KRISTINA WAYBORN, KABIR BEDI
Produced by ALBERT R. BROCCOLI
Directed by JOHN GLEN
Screenstory & Screenplay by GEORGE MacDONALD FRASER
and RICHARD MAIBAUM
& MICHAEL G. WILSON
Executive Producer MICHAEL G. WILSON
Production Designer PETER LAMONT
Associate Producer TOM PEVSNER
DISTRIBUTED BY
MGM/UA
ENTERTAINMENT CO.

OCTOPUSSY

The title 'Octopussy' comes from the Ian Fleming collection of short stories Octopussy and The Living Daylights. The two short stories were published shortly after Fleming's death and hardly any of the plots of the short story "Octopussy" is used. The scene at Sotheby's is, however, drawn from the short story "The Property of a Lady" (included in 1967 and later editions of the collection), while Kamal Khan's reaction following the backgammon game is taken from Fleming's novel Moonraker.

George MacDonald Fraser was hired to work on an early draft of the script and he proposed that the story be set in India.

The producers were initially reluctant to feature Maud Adams again because her previous character was killed in The Man with the Golden Gun. Sybil Danning was announced in Prevue magazine in 1982 as being Octopussy, but was never actually cast and Faye Dunaway was deemed too expensive. Finally, Cubby Broccoli gave in and announced that they would re-cast Swedish-born Maud Adams, darken her hair, and change a few lines about how she was raised by an Indian family. A different plotline, with Adams' British father exposed as a traitor, was used instead. As for Adams, she asked to play Octopussy as a European woman and was granted this, but on the title character's name, she felt the producers "went too far".

Octopussy is also the first film to feature Robert Brown as M, following the death of Bernard Lee in 1981 and Desmond Llewelyn got a larger role as Q in this film. One of Bond's allies was played by Vijay Amritraj, who was a professional tennis player. His character not only shares the same first name with him, but he is also a tennis instructor. He uses a tennis racket as a weapon during the auto rickshaw chase, which is accompanied by the sound of a tennis ball being hit and scenes of onlookers turning their heads left and right as if they are watching a tennis match.

Filming of Octopussy began on August the 10th, 1982, with the scene in which Bond arrives at Checkpoint Charlie. Principal photography was done by Arthur Wooster and his second unit, who later filmed the knife-throwing scenes. Much of the film was shot in Udaipur, India, with the Monsoon Palace serving as the exterior of Kamal Khan's palace, while scenes set at Octopussy's palace were filmed at the Lake Palace and Jag Mandir. Bond's hotel was the Shiv Niwas Palace.

When production returned to England, RAF Northolt, RAF Upper Heyford, and RAF Oakley were the main locations. The Karl-Marx-Stadt railways scenes were shot at the Nene Valley Railway, near Peterborough, while studio work was performed at the 007 Stage at Pinewood.

The pre-title sequence has a scene where Bond flies a nimble Bede BD-5J aircraft through an open hangar. Hollywood stunt pilot and aerial co-ordinator J.W. "Corkey" Fornof, who piloted the aircraft at more than 150 miles per hour, has said, "Today, few directors would consider such a stunt. They'd just whip it up in a computer lab."

Having collapsible wings, the plane was shown hidden in a horse trailer, however, it was still a fraction to big and so a dummy was used for this shot. Filming inside the hangar was achieved by attaching the aircraft to an old Jaguar car with a steel pole, driving with the roof removed. The second unit were able to add enough obstacles including people and objects inside the hangar to hide the car and the pole and make it look as though it was actually Moore flying inside the base. For the explosion after the mini jet escapes, however, a miniature of the hangar was constructed and filmed up close. The exploding pieces of the hangar were in reality only four inches in length.

Stunt coordinator Martin Grace suffered an injury while shooting the scene where Bond climbs down the train to catch Octopussy's attention. During the second day of filming, Grace, who was Roger Moore's stunt double for the scene, carried on doing the scene longer than he should have, due to a miscommunication with the second unit director, and the train entered a section of the track which the team had not properly surveyed. Shortly afterwards, a concrete pole fractured Grace's left leg.

The bicyclist seen passing in the middle of a swordfight during the tuk-tuk chase sequence was in fact a bystander who passed through the shot, oblivious to the filming. His intrusion was captured by two cameras and left in the final film.

The Fabergé egg in the film is real; it was made in 1897 and is called the Coronation Egg, although the egg in the film is named in the auction catalogue as "Property of a Lady", which is the name of one of Ian Fleming's short stories released in more recent editions of the collection Octopussy and The Living Daylights.

Octopussy's premiere took place at the Odeon Leicester Square on the 6th of June, 1983, in the company of Prince Charles and Diana, Princess of Wales. Within five months of its premiere, it was released in 16 countries worldwide. The film earned slightly less than For Your Eyes Only, but still grossed $187,500,000, with $67.8 million in the United States alone.

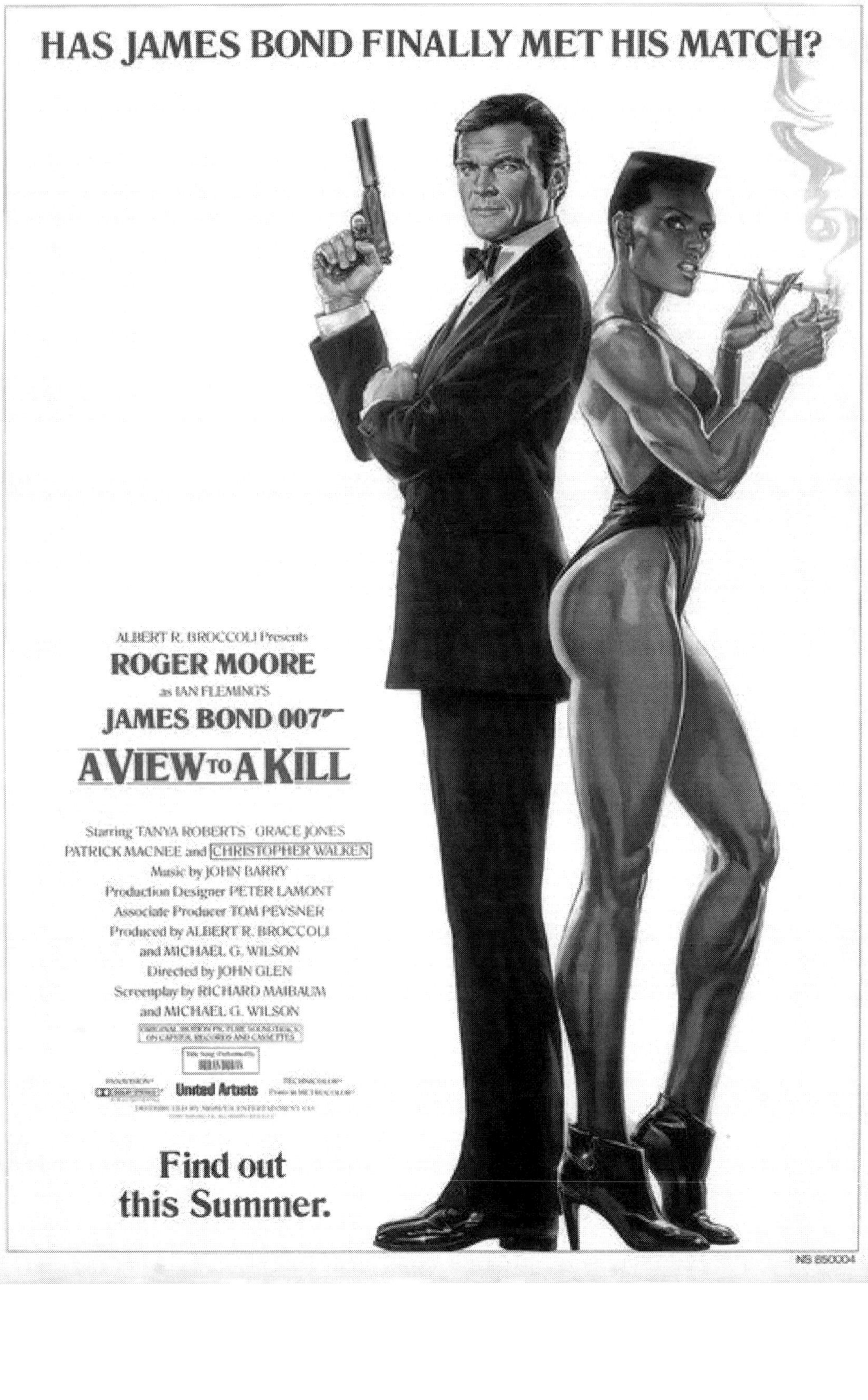
HAS JAMES BOND FINALLY MET HIS MATCH?
ALBERT R. BROCCOLI Presents
ROGER MOORE
as IAN FLEMING'S
JAMES BOND 007
A VIEW TO A KILL
Starring TANYA ROBERTS GRACE JONES
PATRICK MACNEE and CHRISTOPHER WALKEN
Music by JOHN BARRY
Production Designer PETER LAMONT
Associate Producer TOM PEVSNER
Produced by ALBERT R. BROCCOLI
and MICHAEL G. WILSON
Directed by JOHN GLEN
Screenplay by RICHARD MAIBAUM
and MICHAEL G. WILSON
United Artists
Find out
this Summer.
NS 850004

A VIEW TO A KILL

A View to a Kill was the next Bond film to hit the screens. It was produced by Cubby Broccoli and Michael G. Wilson with Wilson co-authoring the screenplay.

At the end of Octopussy during the "James Bond Will Return" sequence, it listed the next film as "From a View to a Kill", the name of the original short story, however, the title was later shortened to "A View to a Kill". It was also discovered shortly before the film's release that there was in fact a company with a name similar to Zorin (the Zoran Corporation) in the United States so a disclaimer was added to the start of the film affirming that Zorin was not related to any real-life company.

Early publicity announcements for the film had stated that David Bowie would play the role of Zorin, but he later turned the part down stating that he "didn't want to spend five months watching my stunt double fall off cliffs." The role was later offered to Sting and finally to Christopher Walken who accepted the part.

Grace Jones's bodyguard and boyfriend at the time, Dolph Lundgren, had been visiting set during filming on one occasion. That day an extra was missing so the director, John Glen, asked him if he wanted to get a shot at it. Lundgren appears during the confrontation between Gogol and Zorin at the racetrack, standing several steps below Gogol. The acting bug must have caught him and a year later, Lundgren would shoot to fame starring alongside Sylvester Stallone in Rocky IV.

Production of the A View to a Kill began on the 23rd of June, 1984, in Iceland, where the second unit filmed the pre-title sequence. A week later, several leftover canisters of petrol used during the filming of Ridley Scott's Legend caused Pinewood Studios' "007 Stage" to burn to the ground. The stage was rebuilt, and reopened in January of 1985. It was renamed as "Albert R. Broccoli's 007 Stage" but the Pinewood filming of A View to a Kill had to be done on other stages at the studio. The crew then departed for shooting the horse-racing scenes at Royal Ascot Racecourse. The scene in which Bond and Sutton enter the mineshaft was then filmed in a waterlogged quarry near Staines and the Amberley Chalk Pits Museum in West Sussex.

On October the 6th, 1984, the fourth unit, headed by special effects supervisor John Richardson, began its work on the climactic fight sequence. At first, only a few plates constructed to resemble the Golden Gate Bridge were used. Later that night, shooting of the burning San Francisco City Hall commenced with the first actual scenes atop the bridge filmed the following day.

In Paris it was planned that two stunt men, B.J. Worth and Don Caldvedt, would help film two takes of a parachute drop off a (clearly visible) platform that extended from a top edge of the Eiffel Tower. However, sufficient footage was obtained from Worth's jump, so Caldvedt was told he would not be performing his own jump. Caldvedt, unhappy at not being able to perform the jump, parachuted off the tower in defiance He was subsequently sacked by the production team for jeopardizing the continuation of filming in the city.

The airship used in the climax of the film was a Skyship 500, then on a promotional tour of Los Angeles after its participation in the opening ceremony of the 1984 Olympic Games. At that time, it had "WELCOME" painted across the side of the hull, but that was painted over with "ZORIN INDUSTRIES" for the film. After filming A View to a Kill the ship was again painted, this time green and red, as a part of Fujifilm's blimp fleet. In real life, inflating it would take up to 24 hours, but during the film it was shown to take just two minutes.

The opening night of A View to a Kill was on the 22nd of May, 1985, at the San Francisco Palace of Fine Arts. It was the first Bond films not too have a U.K. premiere. The British premiere was held on the 12th of June, 1985, at the Odeon Leicester Square Cinema in London. It achieved a box office collection of $152.4 million worldwide with $50.3 million in the United States alone. On its opening weekend in the US it earned $10.6 million. Despite the big numbers it was not the financial success Eon and United Artists had hoped for.

With the release of A View to a Kill also came the end of Roger Moore as James Bond. He had fulfilled his three-film contract long ago and had remained on as Bond film by film. Moore was now 57 years of age and had played Bond for 7 films over 12 years. He had originally planned on leaving the franchise after For Your Eyes Only, but had remained on for Octopussy with the news that McClory was making a rival film, as Cubby knew that changing their leading man at such a time could have a negative impact. He had then decided to stay on one last time for A View to a Kill but now the search for the next Bond was on.

SO CLOSE

A couple of years previously, on the set of For Your Eyes Only, a Bond girl played by the late Casey Brosnan had been working. During her off screen time her husband, Pierce, had been visiting set and he had got to know the film's producers through that. When the search appeared for the next Bond, Pierce's name came up top of the list. The timing appeared good. It was 1986 and Pierce had just finished a series of shows he had been working on called Remington Steele. He auditioned for the show and the part was his. But there was a problem. Pierce's contract for Remington Steele meant that despite there being an end to the series he had a 60 day lay-down period during which the show could be re-sold and re-instated at any time. If the rights to Remington Steele were brought by someone else his contract would have pulled him away from Bond and that was a huge gamble to take with a multi-million dollar movie project. Despite this Broccoli, and his now new partner on the films stepson Michael Wilson, were determined to have Pierce as the next Bond. With some rescheduling they made it seem possible. With the 60-day lay down period ticking away photoshoots took place with Pierce portraying and preparing for his new role as Bond. Press releases were made. Then came the final day. Day 60. Suddenly the telephone rings and Brosnan looks at it. He picks the phone up and hears the news he dreads. NBC have brought the rights to Remington Steele and Pierce's contract to play the lead role along with it. Unsuprisingly Remington Steele had become more popular with the news that its lead actor, Brosnan, would be Bond. With the series re-starting and preventing him from being Bond, the interest in the show dwindled once again resulting in only five further episodes being filmed. Such is the hindsight of television producers? In an instant, Pierce Brosnan was snatched from the role and the search for a new Bond was back on.

Auditions were implemented. Amongst them was Sam Neill. Then unknown, Bond co-producer Michael G. Wilson, director John Glen, and Dana and Barbara Broccoli very much liked Sam for the role but Cubby was not persuaded. Eventually the part was won by Timothy Dalton. A Welsh actor, established in Shakespearian theatre. Not your typical Bond. Timothy had felt that the previous movies had lost their passion for Bond. Fleming's books had created Bond as a tough guy and a cold-hearted killer. The previous films had been a little more comedic and witty. The audience had enjoyed that but Dalton wanted to bring back the Bond of old. Tough and ruthless. This all sounded great, but in reality it was not what the audience wanted. License to Kill was to become a very dark and violent picture. The most violent Bond film to date. This was how the books were but not how cinema goers seemed to want Bond.

THE NEW JAMES BOND . . . LIVING ON THE EDGE
007
ALBERT R. BROCCOLI
presents
TIMOTHY DALTON
as IAN FLEMING'S
JAMES BOND 007
THE LIVING DAYLIGHTS

THE LIVING DAYLIGHTS

Originally The Living Daylights, was proposed to be a prequel to the series (much as 2006's Casino Royale would later be) showing Bond in his early days and becoming the man he is, but this idea was laid aside and the plot rewritten. SMERSH's acronym from Fleming's novel's Smiert Shpionam – "Death to spies" – would form the storyline.

In the autumn of 1985, following the financial and critical disappointment of A View to a Kill, work began on scripts for the next Bond film, with the knowledge that Roger Moore would not reprise the role of James Bond.

Maryam d'Abo, a former model, was cast as the Czechoslovakian cellist Kara Milovy. In 1984, d'Abo had attended auditions for the role of Pola Ivanova in A View To a Kill but did not get the part. Barbara Broccoli, however, remembered her and auditioned her for the part of d'Abo instead.

Originally, the KGB general set up by Koskov was to be General Gogol; however, Walter Gotell was too sick to handle the major role, and so the character of Leonid Pushkin replaced Gogol, who then appears only briefly at the end of the film. This was Gogol's final appearance in a James Bond film.

The Living Daylights was shot at Pinewood Studios on the 007 stage, as well as Wissensee in Austria. The pre-title sequence was filmed on the Rock of Gibraltar and although the sequence shows a hijacked Land Rover careering down various sections of road for several minutes before bursting through a wall towards the sea, the location mostly used the same short stretch of road at the very top of the Rock, shot from numerous different angles. The beach defences seen at the foot of the Rock in the initial shot were also added solely for the film, to an otherwise non-military area. The action involving the Land Rover switched from Gibraltar to Beachy Head in the U.K. for the shot showing the vehicle actually getting airborne. Trial runs of the stunt with the Land Rover, during which Bond escapes by parachute from the tumbling vehicle, were filmed in the Mojave Desert although the final cut of the film uses a shot achieved using a dummy. Other locations included Germany, the United States, and Italy, while the desert scenes were shot in Ouarzazate, Morocco. The conclusion of the film was shot at the Schönbrunn Palace in Vienna and Elveden Hall in Suffolk.

Principle photography commenced in Gibraltar on the 17th of September, 1986. Aerial stuntmen B. J. Worth and Jake Lombard performed the pre-credits parachute jump. Both the terrain and wind were unfavourable and consideration was given to the stunt being done using cranes but aerial stunts arranger B. J. Worth stuck to skydiving and completed the scenes in a day. The aircraft used for the jump was a C-130 Hercules, which in the film had M's office installed in the aircraft cabin. The initial point of view for the scene shows M in what appears to be his usual London office, but the camera then zooms out to reveal that it is, in fact, inside an aircraft. Although marked as a Royal Air Force aircraft, the one used actually belonged to the Spanish Air Force and was used again later in the film for the Afghanistan sequences (but this time repainted with "Russian" markings).

The Living Daylights also reunited Bond with Aston Martin, this time in the form of a V8 Vantage. Two different Aston Martin models were used in filming, a V8 Volante convertible, and later for the Czechoslovakia scenes, a hard-top non-Volante V8 Vantage badged to look like a Volante.

The Prince and Princess of Wales were again top of the list for Bond's U.K. premiere. On the 27th of June, 1987, The Living Daylights premiered at the Odeon Leicester Square in London. The film grossed the equivalent of $191.2 million worldwide. In the United States it earned $51,185,000, including an opening weekend of $11,051,284, far surpassing the $5 million grossed by "The Lost Boys" which was released on the same day.

In the film, Koskov and Whitaker repeatedly use vehicles and drug packets marked with the Red Cross. This action angered a number of Red Cross Societies, who sent letters of protest regarding the film. The British Red Cross attempted to sue Eon Productions and United Artists but eventually, after a disclaimer was added to the start of the film, the case was dropped.

007
TM
ALBERT R. BROCCOLI
Presents
TIMOTHY DALTON
as IAN FLEMING'S
JAMES BOND 007
LICENCE TO KILL
CAREY LOWELL ROBERT DAVI TALISA SOTO ANTHONY ZERBE
ALEC MILLS Production Designer PETER LAMONT Music by MICHAEL KAMEN
PEVSNER and BARBARA BROCCOLI Written by MICHAEL G. WILSON and RICHARD MAIBAUM
Produced by ALBERT R. BROCCOLI and MICHAEL G. WILSON Directed by JOHN GLEN
MGM/UA
CBS FOX

LICENSE TO KILL

Shortly after The Living Daylights was released, Cubby Broccoli and writers Michael G. Wilson and Richard Maibaum started discussing its successor. They wanted the film to retain its darker style towards Bond. For the primary location, the producers wanted a place where the series had not yet visited. Not many places were left although China was visited following an invitation by its government, but the idea fell through partly because of the 1987 film "The Last Emperor" which the producers felt had removed some of the novelty from the country. By this stage the writers had already talked about a chase sequence along the Great Wall, as well as a fight scene amongst the Terracotta Army. Wilson also wrote two plot outlines about a drug lord in the Golden Triangle before the plans fell through. The writers eventually decided on a setting in a tropical country while Broccoli negotiated to film at the Estudios Churubusco in Mexico City. In 1985, the Films Act was passed, removing the Eady Levy, which resulted in foreign artists being taxed more heavily. The associated rising costs to Eon Productions meant no part of Licence to Kill would be filmed in the UK, making it the first Bond film not to do so.

The initial outline of what would become Licence to Kill was drawn up by Wilson and Maibaum. Before the pair could develop the script, the Writers Guild of America (WGA) went on strike and Maibaum was unable to continue writing, leaving Wilson to work on the script on his own. Although both the main plot and title of Licence to Kill owe nothing to any of the Fleming novels, there are elements from the books that are used in the storyline, including a number of aspects of the short story "The Hildebrand Rarity", such as the character Milton Krest. The novel Live and Let Die provided the material surrounding Felix Leiter's mauling by a shark, whilst the later film version of the book provided the close similarity between the main villain, Kananga, and Licence to Kill's main villain Sanchez.

The script, initially called Licence Revoked, was written with Dalton's characterisation of Bond in mind, and the obsession with which Bond pursues Sanchez on behalf of Leiter and his dead wife is seen as being because "of his own brutally cut-short marriage." Dalton's darker portrayal of Bond led to the violence being increased and more graphic. For the location Wilson created the Republic of Isthmus, a banana republic based on Panama, with the evil Sanchez bearing similarities to General Manuel Noriega. The parallels between the two figures were based on Noriega's political use of drug trafficking and money laundering to provide revenues for Panama. Robert Davi suggested the line "loyalty is more important than money", which he felt was fitting to the character of Franz Sanchez, whose actions were noticed by Davi to be concerned with betrayal and retaliation.

Robert Davi was cast as Franz Sanches following a suggestion by Broccoli's daughter Tina, and screenwriter Richard Maibaum, who had seen Davi in the television film Terrorist on Trial: The United States vs. Salim Ajami. To portray Sanchez, Davi researched on the Colombian drug cartels and how to do a Colombian accent, and since he was method acting, he would stay in character off-set. After Davi read Casino Royale for preparation, he decided to turn Sanchez into a "mirror image" of James Bond, based on Ian Fleming's descriptions of Le Chiffre.

Davi later helped out on the casting of Sanchez's mistress Lupe Lamora, by playing Bond in the audition, with Talisa Soto being picked from twelve candidates because Davi expressed he "would kill for her". David Hedison returned to play Felix Leiter, sixteen years after being the agent in Live and Let Die (Hedison was the only actor to play Leiter twice, until Jeffrey Wright appeared in both Casino Royale and Quantum of Solace).

Up-and-coming actor at the time, Benicio Del Toro was chosen to play Sanchez's henchman, Dario for being "laid back while menacing in a quirky sort of way", according to Glen. Wayne Newton got the role of Professor Joe Butcher after sending a letter to the producers expressing interest in a cameo because he always wanted to be in a Bond film. The President of Isthmus was played by Pedro Armendáriz, Jr., the son of the late Pedro Armendariz who had played Ali Kerim Bey in From Russia with Love and who had committed suicide shortly after.

Principle photography ran from the 18th of July to the 18th of November, 1988. Shooting began in Mexico, which mostly doubled for the fictional Republic of Isthmus, with locations in Mexico City included the Biblioteca Del Banco de Mexico for the exterior of El Presidente Hotel and the Casino Español for the interior of Casino de Isthmus whilst the Teatro de la Ciudad was used for its exterior. Villa Arabesque in Acapulco was used for Sanchez's lavish villa, and the La Rumorosa Mountain Pass in Tecate was used as the filming site for the tanker chase during the climax of the film. Sanchez's Olympiatec Meditation Institute was shot at the Otomi Ceremonial Centre in Temoaya. Other underwater sequences were shot at the Isla Mujeres near Cancun.

In August of 1988, production moved to the Florida Keys, notably Key West. Seven Mile Bridge towards Pigeon Key was used for the sequence in which the armoured truck transporting Sanchez, following his arrest, is driven off the edge. Other locations there included Ernest Hemingway House, Key West International Airport, Mallory Square, St. Mary's Star of the Sea Church for Leiter's wedding and Stephano's House was 707 South Street. The U.S. Coast Guard Pier was used to film Isthmus City Harbour.

The scene where Sanchez's plane is hijacked was filmed on location in Florida, with stuntman Jake Lombard jumping from a helicopter to a plane and Dalton himself being filmed atop the aircraft. The plane towed by the helicopter was a life-sized model created by special effects supervisor John Richardson. After filming wide shots of David Hedison and Dalton parachuting, closer shots were made near the church location. During one of the takes, a malfunction of the harness equipment caused Hedison to fall on the pavement. The injury made him limp for the remainder of filming.

The underwater battle between Bond and the henchmen required two separate units. One a surface team led by Arthur Wooster which used Dalton himself, and an underwater one which involved experienced divers. The barefoot water-skiing was done by world champion Dave Reinhart, with some close-ups using Dalton on a special rig. Milton Krest's death used a prosthetic head which was created by John Richardson's team based on a mould of Anthony Zerbe's face. The result was so gruesome that it was shortened and toned down for the final version to avoid censorship problems.

For the climactic tanker chase, the producers used an entire section of a highway near Mexicali, which had been closed for safety reasons. Sixteen 18-wheeler tankers were used, some with modifications made by manufacturer Kenworth at the request of driving stunts arranger Remy Julienne. Most were given improvements to their engines to run faster, while one model had an extra steering wheel on the back of the cabin so a hidden stuntman could drive while Carey Lowell was in the front and another received extra suspension on its back so it could lift its front wheels. Although a rig was constructed to help one truck tilt onto its side, it was not necessary as Julienne was able to pull off the stunt without the aid of camera trickery

Shortly before release of License To Kill, film ratings organisations had objections to the excessive and realistic violence, with both the Motion Picture Association of America and the British Board of Film Classification requesting content adaptations. The BBFC in particular demanded the cut of 36 seconds of film. The 2006 Ultimate Edition DVD of Licence to Kill marked the first release of the film without those cuts.

Licence to Kill premiered at the Odeon Leicester Square in London on June the 13th, 1989, raising £200,000 for The Prince's Trust charity on the night. The film grossed a total of £7.5 million in the United Kingdom, making it the seventh most successful film of the year, despite gaining a '15' certificate rating. Worldwide it made $156 million, making it the twelfth biggest box-office draw of the year. The U.S. cinema returns though were only $34.6 million, making Licence to Kill the least financially successful James Bond film in the U.S. (when accounting for inflation). A factor suggested for the poor takings were fierce competition at the cinema, with Licence to Kill released alongside some other huge films such as Lethal Weapon 2, Indiana Jones and the Last Crusade and Batman.

There were also issues with the promotion of the film: promotional material in the form of teaser posters created by Bob Peak, based on the Licence Revoked title and commissioned by Broccoli, had been produced, but MGM decided against using them after American test screenings showed 'Licence Revoked' to be a common American phrase for the withdrawal of a driving license. The delayed and corrected advertising by Steven Chorney, in the traditional style, limited the film's pre-release screenings. MGM also discarded a campaign created by advertising executive Don

Smolen, who had worked in the publicity campaign for eight previous Bond films before, emphasizing the rougher content of the movie.

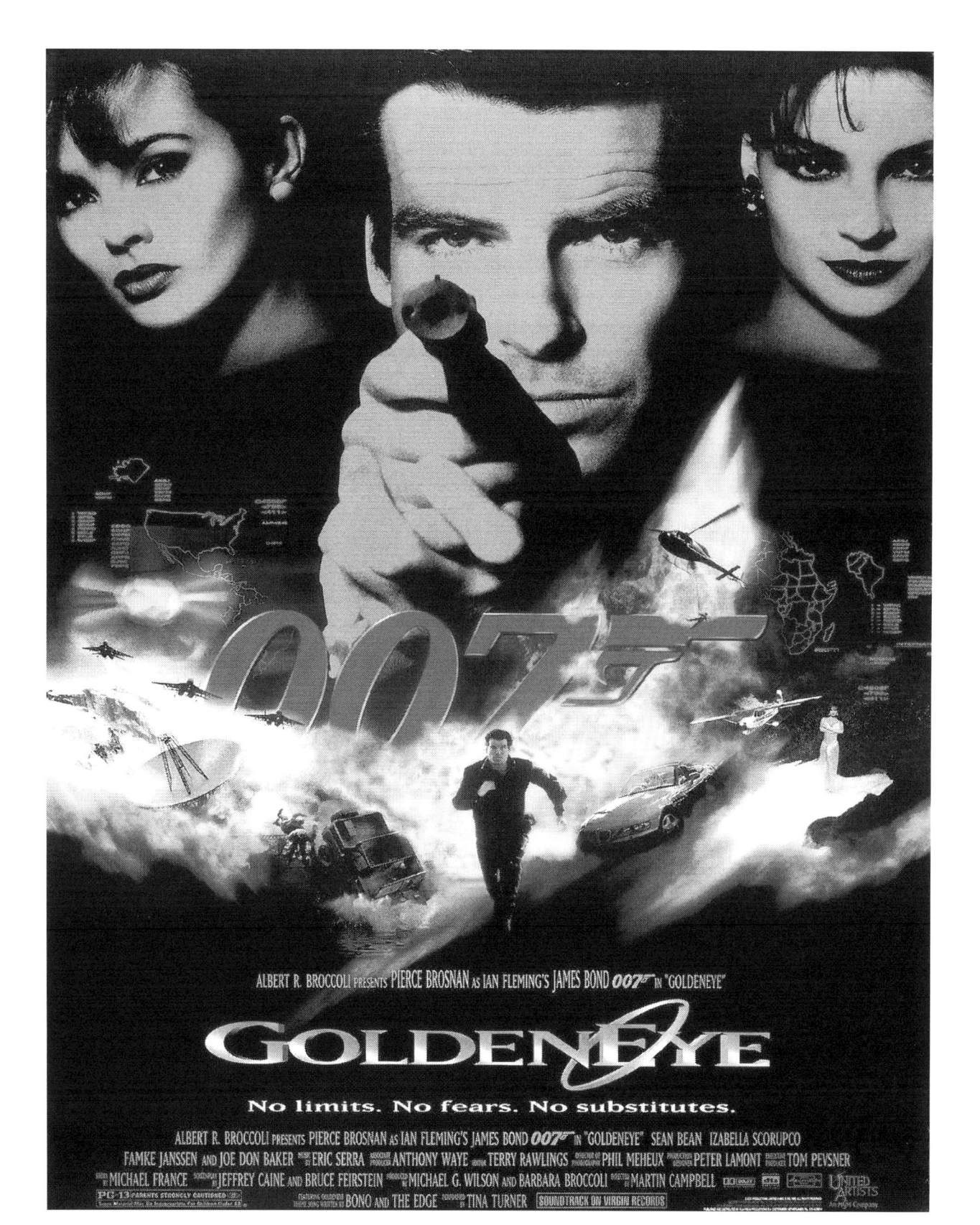

GOLDENEYE

No limits. No fears. No substitutes.

ALBERT R. BROCCOLI presents PIERCE BROSNAN as IAN FLEMING'S JAMES BOND 007 in "GOLDENEYE" SEAN BEAN IZABELLA SCORUPCO FAMKE JANSSEN and JOE DON BAKER music by Eric Serra associate producer ANTHONY WAYE editor TERRY RAWLINGS director of photography PHIL MEHEUX production designer PETER LAMONT executive producer TOM PEVSNER story by MICHAEL FRANCE screenplay by JEFFREY CAINE and BRUCE FEIRSTEIN produced by MICHAEL G. WILSON and BARBARA BROCCOLI directed by MARTIN CAMPBELL

FEATURING GOLDENEYE THEME SONG WRITTEN BY BONO AND THE EDGE PERFORMED BY TINA TURNER SOUNDTRACK ON VIRGIN RECORDS

GOLDENEYE

Timothy Dalton's two attempts at James Bond were perfect... But perfect for the books. Along with the dark new films audience numbers declined and to make things worse, with United Artists now owning 50% of Bond, the films became a pawn in negotiations and Wall Street.

Bond went on hiatus for 6 years and fans began wondering if that was the end. Even Cubby believed there would be no more, at least not in his lifetime. With financial constraints from his studio partners and the constant hindrance of United Artists interfering in the making of the films, Cubby decided to call it a day. He decided to put the Bond rights up for sale.

With the fear of losing Bond forever, United Artists realized they had to do something to prevent Cubby selling up. They negotiated with Cubby Broccoli and put the right people in the right places to help him make the films he wanted.

Bond had been off of the screen for so long even the Wall Street Journal had described the news of a new Bond movie as "a $50 million gamble". The Cold War was at an end and there was a serious doubt that even Bond could survive in this new post-war world. Despite this the go-ahead was given.

Pre-production work for the third James Bond film starring Timothy Dalton, fulfilling his three-film contract, began in May of 1990. A poster for the then-upcoming movie was even featured on the Carlton Hotel during the 1990 Cannes Film Festival. In August Eon Productions parted company with writer Richard Maibaum, who had worked on the scripts of all but three Bond films so far, and director John Glen, responsible for the previous five instalments of the series. Broccoli listed among the possible directors John Landis, Ted Kotcheff, and John Byrum. Michael G. Wilson contributed a script, and Wiseguy co-producer Alfonse Ruggiero Jr. was hired to rewrite. Production was set to start in 1990 in Hong Kong for a planned release in late 1991.

With a script virtually ready and just a director to find, the project entered development hell. Legal problems between Metro-Goldwyn-Mayer, parent company of the series' distributor United Artists, and Danjaq/Eon surfaced. In 1990 MGM/UA had been purchased by French-Italian broadcasting group Pathé. Pathé CEO Giancarlo Parretti intended to sell off the distribution rights of the studio's catalogue so he could collect advance payments to finance the buyout. This included international broadcasting rights to the 007 library at cut-rate prices, leading Danjaq to sue, alleging the licensing violated the Bond distribution agreements the company made with United Artists back in 1962, while negating Danjaq a share of the profits. This led to two years of litigation, during which time, Dalton's deal with Eon to play Bond expired.

In May of the following year, MGM announced that Bond was back in play and a seventeenth James Bond film was to be based on a screenplay by Michael France.

After Michael France delivered the original screenplay, Jeffrey Caine was brought in to rewrite it. Caine kept many of France's ideas but added the prologue prior to the credits. Kevin Wade polished the script and Bruce Feirstein added the finishing touches. In the film, the writing credit was shared by Caine and Feirstein, while France was credited with only the story, an arrangement he felt was unfair, particularly as he believed the additions made were not an improvement on his original version. Wade did not receive an official credit, but was acknowledged in the naming of Jack Wade, the CIA character he had created.

All that was needed was a new James Bond. The role this time was not advertised as such. Pierce Brosnan had been the man for the job once before but fate had snatched him from the role. This time around he would be free of contract and so the role was offered to Pierce.

The casting of Pierce Brosnan as Bond was Cubby Broccoli's last input into James Bond. From that moment, already in his 80's and very unwell, Cubby handed the reigns over to his two children. Michael Wilson, his stepson who had already been co-producing Bond since Saltzman left, and daughter Barbara Broccoli. The weight of Bond was now bearing down on their shoulders.

Six months after the release of Goldeneye, Barbara Broccoli had been having lunch in a Hollywood restaurant. Sat on a table nearby had been Sean Connery. It was now public knowledge now that Cubby was very ill. He was 87 at this time and the end was nearing. Sean stood from his table, walked over to Barbara and said "I would like to speak to him". This was a man who had almost a personal vendetta against Cubby for years, yet suddenly he showed compassion. A shocked Barbara called her father on the phone straight away and Sean and Cubby spoke for the first time in almost thirty years. Cubby said to Sean "we made something pretty special together, I love you". Sean replied "I love you".

Days later the sad news came. Cubby had passed away. The film industry mourned, the fans shed a tear, and a part of James Bond vanished.

Pierce was accepted by audiences almost immediately. He made a natural Bond and the films became a little lighter once again. Many say they were a little to 'light' with some quite over the top ideas. Bond would have invisible cars and surf on Tsunami's. Many thought this was far too over the top for Bond, verging on the realms of science-fiction, but yet the audiences still loved it.

Pierce Brosnan's relatively low $1.2 million salary also allowed the producers to spend properly the $60 million budget lent by MGM. Judi Dench was cast as the first female M. John Woo was approached as the director, and turned down the opportunity, but said he was honoured by the offer. The producers then chose New Zealander Martin Campbell.

While the story was not based on a work by Ian Fleming, the title GoldenEye had been named after Fleming's Jamaican estate where he had written the Bond novels.

Although only six years since the release of Licence to Kill, world politics had changed dramatically in the interim. The Berlin Wall had fallen. The Soviet Union had collapsed and the Cold War era was all but a shadow of the past.

Principle photography for the film began on the 16th of January 1995 and continued until the 6th of June. The producers were unable to film at Pinewood, the usual location for Bond films, because it had been reserved for another film, "First Knight". Instead, an old Rolls-Royce factory at the Leavesden Aerodrome in Hertfordshire was converted into a new studio.

The bungee jump at the beginning of the film was shot at the Contra Dam (also known as the Verzasca or Locarno Dam) in Ticino, Switzerland. The film's casino scenes and the Tiger helicopter's demonstration were shot in Monte Carlo. Reference footage for the tank chase was shot on location in St. Petersburg and then matched to the studio at Leavesden. The climactic scenes on the satellite dish were shot at Arecibo Observatory in Puerto Rico and the actual MI6 headquarters were used for external views of M's office. Some of the scenes in St. Petersburg were shot in London, including St. Petersburg Airport which was in fact Epsom Downs Racecourse.

The French Navy provided full use of the frigate FS La Fayette and their newest helicopter, the Eurocopter Tiger to the film's production team. The French government also allowed the use of Navy logos as part of the promotional campaign for the film. However, the producers had a dispute with the French Ministry of Defence over Brosnan's opposition to French nuclear weapons testing and his involvement with Greenpeace. As a result, the French premiere of the film was cancelled.

The sequences involving the armoured train were filmed on the Nene Valley Railway, near Peterborough in the U.K. The train was composed of a British Rail Class 20 diesel-electric locomotive and a pair of BR Mk.1 coaches, all heavily disguised to resemble a Soviet armoured train.

Stunt car coordinator Remy Julienne described the car chase between the Aston Martin DB5 and the Ferrari F355 as between "a perfectly shaped, old and vulnerable vehicle and a race car". The stunt had to be meticulously planned as the cars are vastly different. Nails were attached to the

F355 tyres to make it skid, and during one take of the sliding vehicles, both cars collided. The largest stunt sequence in the film was the tank chase, which took around six weeks to film, partly on location in St. Petersburg and partly at Leavesden. A Russian T-54/55 tank, on loan from the East England Military Museum, was modified with the addition of fake explosive reactive armour panels. In order to avoid destroying the pavement on the city streets of St. Petersburg, the steel off-road tracks of the T-54/55 were replaced with the rubber-shoed tracks from a British Chieftain Tank

GoldenEye was the first film bound by BMW's three picture deal, so the producers were offered BMW's latest roadster, the BMW Z3. For the film, a convertible Z3 is equipped with the usual Q refinements, including a self-destruct feature and Stinger Missiles behind the headlights. The Z3 did not have much screen time though and none of the gadgets were used, which Martin Campbell attributed to the deal with BMW coming in the last stages of production.

GoldenEye premiered on the 13th of November 1995, at the Radio City Music Hall in New York City, and went on general release in the USA on the 17th of November, 1995. The U.K. premiere, attended by Prince Charles, followed on the 22nd of November at the Odeon Leicester Square, with general release two days later.

The film earned over $26 million during its opening across 2,667 cinemas in the USA. Its worldwide sales were around the equivalent of $350 million and it had the fourth highest worldwide gross of all films in 1995. Goldeneye was the most successful Bond film since Moonraker.

ALBERT R. BROCCOLI'S EON PRODUCTIONS PRESENTS PIERCE BROSNAN AS IAN FLEMING'S JAMES BOND 007 IN
007
Tomorrow Never Dies
ALBERT R. BROCCOLI'S EON PRODUCTIONS PRESENTS PIERCE BROSNAN AS IAN FLEMING'S JAMES BOND 007 IN "TOMORROW NEVER DIES" JONATHAN PRYCE MICHELLE YEOH TERI HATCHER
JOE DON BAKER AND JUDI DENCH COSTUME DESIGNER LINDY HEMMING MUSIC BY DAVID ARNOLD DIRECTOR OF PHOTOGRAPHY ROBERT ELSWIT PRODUCTION DESIGNER ALLAN CAMERON LINE PRODUCER ANTHONY WAYE
WRITTEN BY BRUCE FEIRSTEIN PRODUCED BY MICHAEL G. WILSON AND BARBARA BROCCOLI DIRECTED BY ROGER SPOTTISWOODE
PG-13
TITLE SONG PERFORMED BY SHERYL CROW

TOMORROW NEVER DIES

Following the success of Goldeneye in reviving the Bond series, there had been pressure to recreate that success in the film's follow-up production. This pressure came not only from MGM but also its new owner, billionaire Kirk Kerkorian. Kirk wanted for the film's release to coincide with MGM's public stock offering.

The rush to complete the film drove the budget to an astonishing $110 million. The producers were unable to convince Martin Campbell, the director of GoldenEye, to return. His agent said that "Martin just didn't want to do two Bond films in a row." Instead, Roger Spittiswoode was chosen in September of 1996. Spottiswoode had previously offered to direct a Bond film back when Timothy Dalton was in the leading role but had declined at the time.

As had been the case with several previous films in the series, an entirely original story was required as there remained no more Fleming novels or stories to adapt. The scriptwriting process was finished very late due to lengthy disputes. Spottiswoode claimed that MGM had a script in January of 1997 revolving round Hong Kong's transfer of sovereignty to China, however, this plot could not be used for a film opening at the end of the year so a new storyline had to be thought up.

Writer Donald E. Westlake came up with the new plot with Bruce Feirstein (who had worked on Goldeneye) penning the first script draft. Feirstein claimed that his inspiration was his own experience working with journalism, stating that he aimed to "write something that was grounded in a nightmare of reality". Feirstein's script was then passed to Spottiswoode who reworked it before gathering seven Hollywood screenwriters in London to brainstorm, eventually choosing Nicholas Meyer to perform further rewrites. The script was also worked on by Dan Petrie, Jr. and David Campbell Wilson before Feirstein, who retained the sole writing credit, was brought in for a final polish. While many reviewers compared Elliot Carver to Rupert Murdoch, Feirstein based the character on Robert Maxwell. There is a reference to the mogul's death when M instructs Moneypenny to issue a press release stating that Carver died "falling overboard on his yacht."

The title for the film was inspired by the Beatles' song "Tomorrow Never Knows". Eventually the title became "Tomorrow Never Lies" (referring to the Tomorrow newspaper in the plot) and when this was faxed to MGM, through an error, the film title was read as "Tomorrow Never Dies". MGM liked this new title and insisted on it being used.

For the role of Paris Carver, actress Sela Ward was auditioned for the role. She narrowly lost out on the role as producers said that had she been ten years younger she would have been perfect for it. Eventually the role went to Teri Hatcher. Teri was three months pregnant when shooting started and scenes had to be cut in such a way as to not show this.

For the part of Elliot Carver, producers initially offered the part to Anthony Hopkins (Hopkins had also been offered a part in Goldeneye) but he rejected it. Jonathon Pryce was then offered the part.

Natasha Henstridge had been considered for the lead Bond Girl part, but eventually this went to Michelle Yeoh and the character of Wai Lin, a Chinese spy was created.

German actor, Gotz Otto was cast for the role of Elliot Carver's henchman, Richard Stamper, after an impressive audition. He was given twenty seconds to introduce himself; his hair had recently been cropped short for a TV role. Saying, "I'm big, I'm bad, and I'm German", he got the part in five

With casting accomplished, second unit filming began on the 18th of January, 1997, with Vic Armstrong directing. Vic is an accomplished stunt man/coordinator having done dozens of Bond stunts over the years. When he started out on his career, his first Bond stunt had been as the first first Ninja abseiling into Blofeld's volcano in You Only Live Twice. The pre-credits sequence was filmed at Peyresourde Airport in the French Pyrenees before the crew moved on to Portsmouth to film the scenes where the Royal Navy prepares to engage the Chinese. The main unit began filming on the 1st of April. They were unable to use the Leavesden Film Studios, which they had constructed from an abandoned Rolls-Royce factory for GoldenEye, as this time George Lucas had poached it first for filming Star Wars Episode I: The Phantom Menace. Instead they constructed sound stages in another derelict industrial site nearby. The 007 Stage at Pinewood was also used. The scene at the "U.S. Air Base in the South China Sea" where Bond hands over the GPS encoder was actually filmed in the area known as Blue Section at RAF Lakenheath. The sea landing used the vast tank which had been built for Titanic in Rosarito, Mexico. The studios had managed to obtain a visa to film in Ho Chi Minh City, Vietnam, but the Vietnamese were unhappy with the crew and equipment needed for pyrotechnics so they withdrew permission at the last moment. Instead, Bangkok in Thailand was used for the scenes.

Two locations from previous Bond films were used: Brosnan and Hatcher's love scene was filmed at Stoke Park, which had been featured in Goldfinger, and the bay where they search for Carver's stealth boat is Phang Nga Bay, Thailand, previously used for The Man with the Golden Gun.

Spottiswoode tried to innovate in the action scenes. At the last moment he came up with the scenes involving Bond and Wai Lin on a BMW motorcycle and another innovation was the remote-controlled car, which had no visible driver (an effect achieved by adapting a BMW 750i to put the steering wheel

on the back seat). The car chase sequence with the 750i took three weeks to film at Brent Cross shopping centre car park in London. One stunt involving setting fire to three vehicles. This produced more smoke than anticipated, causing a member of the public to call the fire services.

Not all on set ran smoothly. Spottiswoode and Feirstein were no longer on speaking terms at one point and crew members had threatened to resign, with one saying "All the happiness and teamwork which is the hallmark of Bond has disappeared completely."

Tomorrow Never Dies marked the first appearance of the Walther P99 as Bond's pistol. It replaced the Walther PPK that the character had carried in every Eon Bond film since Dr. No in 1962, with the exception of Moonraker in which Bond never got to use a pistol. Walther wanted to debut its new firearm in a Bond film, which had been one of its most visible endorsers. Bond would use the P99 until Daniel Craig reverted back to the PPK in Quantum of Solace.

Tomorrow Never Dies had a World Charity Premiere at The Odeon Leicester Square on the 9th of December, 1997. This was followed by an after premiere party at Bedford Square, home of original Ian Fleming publisher, Jonathan Cape. The film went on general release in the UK and Iceland on December the 12th and in most other countries the following week. It opened at number 2 in the US, with $25,143,007 from 2,807 cinemas behind Titanic, which would become one of the highest-grossing films of its time. Tomorrow Never Dies ultimately achieved a worldwide gross of over $330 million, although it did not surpass its predecessor Goldeneye, which grossed almost $20 million more.

Nothing can equal James Bond

ALBERT R. BROCCOLI'S EON PRODUCTIONS
PRESENTS PIERCE BROSNAN
AS IAN FLEMING'S JAMES BOND 007 IN

The WORLD Is Not Enough
007

ALBERT R. BROCCOLI'S EON PRODUCTIONS PRESENTS PIERCE BROSNAN AS IAN FLEMING'S JAMES BOND 007 IN "THE WORLD IS NOT ENOUGH"
SOPHIE MARCEAU   ROBERT CARLYLE   DENISE RICHARDS   ROBBIE COLTRANE AND JUDI DENCH
MUSIC BY DAVID ARNOLD   PRODUCTION DESIGNER PETER LAMONT
SCREENPLAY BY NEAL PURVIS & ROBERT WADE AND BRUCE FEIRSTEIN
PRODUCED BY MICHAEL G. WILSON AND BARBARA BROCCOLI
DIRECTED BY MICHAEL APTED

© 2001 - Stéphane TRON - http://007art.free.fr

THE WORLD IS NOT ENOUGH

Both Joe Dante and Peter Jackson were considered for the opportunity to direct the next Bond film. Barbara Broccoli had enjoyed Jackson's Heavenly Creatures, and a screening of The Frighteners was arranged for her. She disliked the latter film, however, and showed no further interest in Jackson for Bond after that.

The pre-title sequence lasts for about 14 minutes, the longest pre-title sequence in the Bond series to date. Director Michael Apted said that the scene was originally much longer than that. Originally, the pre-credits sequence was to have ended with Bond's leap from the window and descent to the ground, finishing as Bond rushes away from the area as police cars approach. Then, after the credits the sequence in MI6 headquarters would have been next, with the boat scenes the next major action sequence. However, the pre-credits scenes were viewed as lacklustre when compared to ones from previous 007 films, so the credits were pushed back to appear after the boat sequence.

Initially the film was to be released in 2000, rumoured to be titled Bond 2000. Other rumoured titles included Death Waits for No Man, Fire and Ice, Pressure Point and Dangerously Yours. The title The World Is Not Enough is an English translation of the Latin phrase Orbis non sufficit, which in real life was the motto of Sir Thomas Bond. In the novel On Her Majesty's Secret Service and its film adaption, this is revealed to be the Bond family motto. The phrase originates from the epitaph of Alexander the Great.

Writers, Neal Purvis and Robert Wade, were hired after their work in Plunkett & Macleane with Dana Stevens doing an uncredited rewrite before Bruce Feirstein, who worked in the previous two films, went through it.

The pre-title sequence begins in Bilbao, Spain, and features the Guggenheim Museum. After the opening scene, the film moves to London, showcasing the SIS Building and the Millennium Dome. Following the title sequence, Eilean Donan Castle in Scotland is used as an MI6 location headquarters. Other locations filmed include Baku, Azerbaijan, the Azerbaijan Oil Rocks and Istanbul, Turkey, where Maiden's Tower is shown.

The interior (and single exterior shot) of L'Or Noir casino in Baku, Azerbaijan, was shot at Halton House, the Officers' Mess of RAF Halton.

RAF Northolt was used to depict the airfield runway in Azerbaijan and Zukovsky's quayside caviar factory was shot entirely at the outdoor water tank at Pinewood.

The exterior of Kazakhstan nuclear facility was shot at the Bardenas Reales, in Navarre, Spain, and the exterior of the oil refinery control centre at the Motorola building in Groundwell, Swindon. The exterior of the oil pipeline was filmed in Cwm Dylie, Snowdonia, in Wales while the production teams shot the oil pipeline explosion in Hankley Common, Elstead, Surrey. The underwater submarine scenes were filmed in The Bahamas.

The World Is Not Enough premiered on the 19th of November, 1999, in the United States and on the 26th of November in the United Kingdom. At that time MGM signed a marketing partnership with MTV, primarily for American youths, who were assumed to have considered Bond as "an old-fashioned secret service agent". As a result MTV broadcast more than 100 hours of Bond-related programmes immediately after the film was released, most being presented by Denise Richards who had played Dr. Christmas in the film.

The film opened at the top of the North American box office with $35.5 million. Its final worldwide gross was $361 million worldwide, with $126 million in the United States alone. It became the highest grossing James Bond film of all time until the release of Die Another Day.

ALBERT R. BROCCOLI'S EON PRODUCTIONS Presents PIERCE BROSNAN as IAN FLEMING'S JAMES BOND 007
DIE ANOTHER DAY
ALBERT R. BROCCOLI'S EON PRODUCTIONS PIERCE BROSNAN IAN FLEMING'S JAMES BOND 007 "DIE ANOTHER DAY" HALLE BERRY
TOBY STEPHENS ROSAMUND PIKE RICK YUNE JOHN CLEESE and JUDI DENCH as "M" LINDY HEMMING DAVID ARNOLD
CHRISTIAN WAGNER DAVID TATTERSALL BSC PETER LAMONT CALLUM McDOUGALL ANTHONY WAYE
NEAL PURVIS & ROBERT WADE MICHAEL G. WILSON and BARBARA BROCCOLI LEE TAMAHORI
dts
www.mgm.com DISTRIBUTED BY MGM DISTRIBUTION CO. www.jamesbond.com

DIE ANOTHER DAY

Principle photography of Die Another Day began on January the 11th, 2002, at Pinewood studios. The film was shot primarily in the U.K, Iceland, Cadiz, Spain, and Maui, Hawaii.

Laird Hamilton, Dave Lalama, and Darrick Doerner, performed the pre-title surfing scene at the surf break known as Jaws in Maui. The scene in which Bond surfs the wave created by Icarus when Graves was attempting to kill Bond was shot on a blue screen and the waves, along with all the glaciers in the scene, are computer-generated The shore shots were filmed in both Cadiz and Newquay, Cornwall. The scenes inside Graves' diamond mine were also filmed in Cornwall, at the Eden Project. The scenes involving the Cuban locations of Havana and the fictional Isla de Lss Organos were filmed at La Caleta, Spain.

Gadgets and other props from every previous Bond film, which had previously been stored in Eon Productions' archives, appear in Q's warehouse in the London Underground. Q mentions that the watch he issues Bond is "your 20th, I believe", a reference to Die Another Day being the 20th Eon-produced Bond film.

Hale Berry was injured during filming when debris from a smoke grenade flew into her eye. The debris had to be removed in a 30-minute operation.

The hangar interior of the "US Air Base in South Korea", shown crowded with Chinook helicopters, was filmed at RAF Odiham in Hampshire, U.K, as were the helicopter interior shots during the Switchblade sequence. These latter scenes, though portrayed in the air, were actually filmed entirely on the ground with the sky background being added in post-production using blue screen techniques. Although the base is portrayed in the film as a U.S. base, all the aircraft and personnel in the scene are were actually British Soldiers and Airmen dressed up. In the film, Switchblades (one-person gliders resembling fighter jets in shape) are flown by Bond and Jinx to stealthily enter North Korea. The Switchblade was based on a workable model called "PHASST" (Programmable High Altitude Single Soldier Transport). Kinetic Aerospace Inc.'s lead designer, Jack McCornack was impressed by director Lee Tamahori's way of conducting the Switchblade scene and commented, "It's brief, but realistic. The good guys get in unobserved, thanks to a fast cruise, good glide performance, and minimal radar signature. It's a wonderful promotion for the PHASST".

Die Another Day had its world premiere on the 18th of November, 2002, at the Royal Albert Hall in London. Queen Elizabeth II and Prince Philip were guests of honour, making it the second Bond film premiere to be attended by the Queen, the first one being You Only Live Twice in 1967. The Royal Albert Hall had a make-over for the screening and had been transformed into an ice palace. Proceeds from the première, about £500,000, were donated to the Cinema and Television Benevolent Fund of which the Queen is patron. On the first day, ticket sales reached £1.2 million. Die Another Day eventually earned $432 million worldwide, becoming the sixth highest grossing film of 2002.

Die Another Day became a controversial subject in eastern Asia. The North Korean government disliked the portrayal of their state as brutal and war-hungry. The South Koreans boycotted 145 theatres where it was released on the 31st of December, 2002, as they were offended by the scene in which an American officer issues orders to the South Korean army in the defence of their homeland, and by a lovemaking scene near a statue of the Buddha. The Jogye Buddhist Order issued a statement that the film was "disrespectful to our religion and does not reflect our values and ethics".

A NEW BREED

With the events of 9/11 and the dawn of a new century, the Broccoli's began to wonder where they could take Bond next. They understood that to avoid fans losing interest, a new direction would be needed… but which way to go? The pair remembered back to when they were younger and Cubby had said "when you have a problem, go back to the books". So that is what they did, starting with the first Bond book Casino Royale. Over the years, the rights to Casino Royale had drifted from one owner to another. It had been the one book that Eon needed but could not quite grasp. Finally, in 1999, Sony Pictures (which now owned the rights) approached MGM with and offer. They would be willing to swap the rights to Casino Royale in exchange for the rights to Spider-man. The deal was agreed and Casino Royale was passed, through United Artists, down to Eon Productions. In 2005, Sony would later buy out MGM Studios and regain the rights to the film, but it was too late… For now, Eon could make Casino Royale.

Pierce Brosnan had also now fulfilled his four-film contract as Bond. It was decided that as part of the shake-up, a younger (Brosnan was now passing 50), more energetic, Bond should be found. The decision was reluctantly made to drop Pierce and commence the search for a new leading man.

To make matters worse, the McClory saga was about to rear its ugly head once again. McClory was doing a deal with Colombia Studios based upon their rights to the original television and film adaption of Casino Royale. They had been trying to package up the rights to both Thunderball and Casino Royale to create a rival James Bond franchise. Not only was this a threat to Eon's Bond but it created a huge legal battle between them. Eon offered numerous times to settle out of court, but McClory consistently rejected their offers. McClory's obsession with Bond continued all the way through the courts.

With the final ruling court case coming up, McClory had been out of the country. On the day of the case, McClory flew back to the U.S. At Customs however, there was a "problem". There were issues with his Visa and McClory was held at the airport forcing him to miss the court case. The Judge continued without him however, and even without McClory, ruled in favour of Eon Productions. Finally McClory was out of the way and Eon could get underway with the next Bond film.

Auditions commenced for a new Bond. More than 200 actors went for the role. Henry Caville almost got the part, but at just 22 years of age he was considered too young for the part.

Against everybody's insistence, Barbara Broccoli cast Daniel Craig as the new James Bond. Daniel did not come from the Brosnan or Moore style of acting. He looked rough and tough more than suave and sophisticated. Many could not imagine him in the role and there was a public uproar. Newspapers slandered Craig and websites popped up with petitions asking for him to be removed from the lead.

Eon continued to support Daniel Craig however. From day one of the release of Casino Royale, opinions immediately changed. Audiences were shocked to see a new style of Bond that worked. Craig was able to portray the character with the same traits that we had come to love over the years, but you could also see what was going on behind his eyes. Bond's emotion and pain. Craig showed the audience the anguish and feelings that had been written about in Fleming's novels but which had been very difficult before to portray on the screen.

ALBERT R. BROCCOLI'S EON PRODUCTIONS PRESENTS DANIEL CRAIG
AS IAN FLEMING'S JAMES BOND 007 IN
CASINO ROYALE
CASINO ROYALE
007
ANIEL CRAIG AS IAN FLEMING'S JAMES BOND 007 IN 'CASINO ROYALE' EVA GREEN MADS MIKKELSEN
LINDY HEMMING DAVID ARNOLD STUART BAIRD, A.C.E. PHIL MEHEUX BSC PETER LAMONT
NEAL PURVIS & ROBERT WADE AND PAUL HAGGIS MICHAEL G. WILSON AND BARBARA BROCCOLI
MARTIN CAMPBELL
FEATURING 'YOU KNOW MY NAME' PERFORMED BY CHRIS CORNELL
COLUMBIA PICTURES

CASINO ROYALE

In March of 2004, Neal Purvis and Robert Wade began writing a screenplay for Casino Royale. The aim was simple. Remain faithful to the book. Director Quentin Tarantino expressed interest in directing an adaptation of Casino Royale, although he did not follow this up with Eon. He had been working alongside the Fleming family on his own version of Casino Royale. His version would have been set in the 1950s like the novel though. He had also wanted to film it in black and white. This idea came to a halt though as Eon gained control of the rights to the film and name.

Martin Campbell was announced as the film's director. Eon believed that they had relied too heavily on CGI effects over the more recent films, particularly Die Another Day, and were keen to accomplish the stunts in Casino Royale "the old fashioned way". In keeping with this drive for more realism, screenwriters Purvis, Wade and Haggis wanted the script to follow as closely as possible to the original 1953 novel, keeping Fleming's darker storyline and characterisation of Bond.

The next important casting was that of the lead Bond Girl, Vesper Lynd. Angelina Jolie and Charlize Theron were "strongly considered" for the role and Belgian actress Cecile de France had also auditioned, but her English accent was not believable enough. Audrey Tautou was also considered, but not chosen because of her role in The Da Vinci Code, which was released in May of 2006. It was announced on the 16th of February, 2006, that Eva Green would play the part.

Principal photography for Casino Royale commenced on January the 3rd, 2006 and concluded on the 20th of July. The film was primarily shot at Barrandov Studios in Prague, with additional location shooting in the Bahamas, Italy, Venice, and the United Kingdom. The shoot concluded at Pinewood Studios. Further shooting in the U.K. also took place on the cricket green at Eton College and Dunsfold Aerodrome (otherwise known as the BBC's Top Gear test track). The Skyfleet S570 aircraft in the film was an ex-British Airways 747-200B G-BDXJ which had its engines removed and was modified for its appearance in the film. The modified aircraft had the outboard engines replaced by external fuel tanks, while the inboard engines were replaced by a mock-up pair of engines on each inboard pylon. The cockpit profile was altered to make the 747 look like a prototype of an advanced airliner. This particular plane has been rented out and appeared in numerous movies over the years such as Red 2. It can clearly be seen in the background of Top Gear TV shows as the crew and guests race around the track.

After initial shooting in Prague, the production moved to the Bahamas. Several locations around New Providence were used for filming during February and March, particularly on Paradise Island. Footage set in Mbale, Uganda, was actually filmed at Black Park, a Country Park in Buckinghamshire. Additional scenes took place at Albany House, an estate owned by golfers Ernie Els and Tiger Woods The crew returned to the Czech Republic in April, and continued there, filming in Prague, Plana and Loket, before completing in the town of Karlovy Vary in May. The main Italian location was Venice, where the majority of the film's ending is set. Other scenes in the latter half of the film were shot in late May and early June at the Villa del Balbianello on the shores of Lake Como.

A recreation of the Body Worlds exhibit provided a setting for one scene in the film. Among the Body Worlds plastinates featured in that scene were the "Poker Playing Trio" (which plays a key role in one scene) and the "Rearing Horse and Rider". The exhibition's developer and promoter, German anatomist Gunther von Hagens, also has a cameo appearance in the film, although only his trademark hat is actually visible on screen. Another cameo in the film came from Richard Branson. Branson had paid the producers to show Bond aboard a Virgin Atlantic aircraft. Also sneaked into the contract was a cameo role. As Bond is about to board his plane, in the background of the shot you can see Richard Branson being searched by airport security. Interestingly if you are ever aboard a British Airways flight and they show Casino Royale, you will notice that the shot of Branson and his plane has been "strategically cut" from all BA copies.

First on the schedule were the scenes on the Madagascar building site, shot in the Bahamas on the site of a derelict hotel which Michael G. Wilson had become acquainted with in 1977 during the filming of The Spy Who Loved Me. Researching into locations he discovered the same disused building site is still there. In the scene, Bond drives a digger toward the building, slamming into the concrete plinth on which Mollaka is running. The stunt team built a model and put forward several ways in which the digger could conceivably take out the concrete, including taking out the pillar underneath. A section of the concrete wall was later removed to fit the digger, and reinforced with steel.

In filming the scene in which the engine thrust of a moving aircraft blows the police car high into the air, second unit directors Ian Lowe, Terry Madden and Alex Witt used a crane with a strong lead cable attached to the rear bumper of the vehicle to move it up and backwards at the moment of full extension and away from the plane.

The sinking of the Venetian house at the climax of the film featured the largest rig ever built for a Bond film. For the scene involving Bond following Vesper into the house undergoing renovation supported by inflatable balloons, a tank was constructed at the 007 stage at Pinewood, consisting of a Venetian piazza and the interior of the three-story dilapidated house. The rig, weighing some 90 tons, incorporated electronics with hydraulic valves which were closely controlled by computer because of the dynamic movement within the system on its two axes. The same computer system also controlled the exterior model which the effects team built to one-third scale to film the building eventually collapsing into the Venetian canal. The model elevator within the rig could be immersed in 19 feet (5.8 m) of water, and used banks of compressors to strictly regulate movement.

At the time of filming, Aston Martin were still in the final phases of designing the DBS so the scene involving the car crash was devised using an Aston Martin DB9 that was especially modified to look like Bond's DBS V12 and reinforced to withstand the impact. Due to the low centre of gravity of the vehicle, stuntmen found it difficult to get the car to lift and roll so an 18-inch (450 mm) ramp had to be implemented on the road tarmac at Millbrook Proving Grounds and Adam Kirley, the stunt driver who performed the stunt, had to use an air cannon located behind the driver's seat to propel the car into a roll at the precise moment of impact. At a speed exceeding 70 mph (113 km/h), the car rotated seven times while being filmed, and was confirmed by the Guinness Book of Records on the 5th of November, 2006, to be a new world record.

On the 14th of November, 2006, Casino Royale premiered at the Odeon Leicester Square, the Odeon West End, and the Empire Theatre, simultaneously. It marked the 60th Royal Film Performance and benefited the Cinema & Television Benevolent Fund (CTBF), whose patron, Queen Elizabeth II, was in attendance with the Duke of Edinburgh.

The film has earned $599,045,960 worldwide. Casino Royale was the 4th highest-grossing film of 2006, and was the highest-grossing instalment of the James Bond series until Skyfall surpassed it in November of 2012.

Upon its release in the United Kingdom Casino Royale broke series records on both opening day (£1.7 million) and opening weekend (£13,370,969). At the end of its box office run, the film had grossed £55.4 million, making it the most successful film of the year in the UK, and as of 2011, the tenth highest grossing film of all time in the country.

On its opening day Casino Royale was on top with $14,741,135, and throughout the weekend grossed a total of $40,833,156, placing it second in the ranking behind Happy Feet of all films. ($41.5 million). However, Casino Royale was playing in 370 fewer cinemas and had a better average ($11,890 per cinema, against $10,918 for Happy Feet). It earned $167,445,960 by the end of its run in North America, making Casino Royale the time the highest grossing film of the series.

In January of 2007, Casino Royale became the first Bond film ever to be shown in mainland Chinese cinemas. The Chinese version was edited before release, with the reference to the Cold War re-dubbed and new dialogue added during the poker scene explaining the process of Texas hold 'em, as the game is less familiar in China. Casino Royale earned approximately $11.7 million in China since its opening on the 30th of January on 468 screens, including a record opening weekend collection for a non-Chinese film, with $1.5 million.

ALBERT R. BROCCOLI'S EON PRODUCTIONS DANIEL CRAIG IAN FLEMING'S JAMES BOND 007
QUANTUM OF SOLACE
ALBERT R. BROCCOLI'S EON PRODUCTION DANIEL CRAIG as IAN FLEMING'S JAMES BOND 007 "QUANTUM OF SOLACE"
MATHIEU AMALRIC • GEMMA ARTERTON • JEFFREY WRIGHT • OLGA KURYLENKO • JESPER CHRISTENSEN and JUDI DENCH LOUISE FROGLEY DAVID ARNOLD MATT CHESSE
ROBERTO SCHAEFER IAN FLEMING NEAL PURVIS & ROBERT WADE and PAUL HAGGIS MICHAEL G. WILSON and BARBARA BROCCOLI MARTIN CAMPBELL
THIS FILM IS NOT YET RATED. FOR FUTURE INFO GO TO FILMRATINGS.COM
NOV007
QuantumOfSolaceMovie.com
COLUMBIA PICTURES

QUANTUM OF SOLACE

In July of 2006, as Casino Royale entered post-production, Eon Productions announced that the next film would be based on an original idea by producer Michael G. Wilson. It was decided beforehand the film would be a direct sequel, to exploit Bond's emotions following Vesper's death in the previous film. Just as Casino Royale's theme was terrorism, the sequel focuses on environmentalism. Roger Mitchell, who directed Daniel Craig in Enduring Love and The Mother, was in negotiations to direct, but opted out because there was no script ready at the time. Sony Entertainment vice-chairman Jeff Blake admitted a production schedule of 18 months was not long enough, and the release date was pushed back to late 2008. Neal Purvis and Robert Wade completed their draft of the script by April 2007, and Paul Haggis, who polished the Casino Royale script, began his rewrite the next month.

In June 2007, Marc Forster was confirmed as director. He was surprised that he was approached for the job, stating he was not a big Bond film fan through the years, and that he would not have accepted the project had he not seen Casino Royale prior to making his decision. He felt Bond had been humanised in that film, arguing since travelling the world had become less exotic since the series' advent, it made sense to focus more on Bond as a character. Born in Germany and raised in Switzerland, Forster was the first Bond director not to come from the British Commonwealth of Nations, although he noted Bond's mother is Swiss, making him somewhat appropriate to handle the British icon. The director collaborated strongly with Barbara Broccoli and Michael G. Wilson, noting they only blocked two very expensive ideas he had.

Haggis, Forster and Wilson rewrote the story from scratch. Haggis said he completed his script two hours before the 2007–2008 Writers Guild of America strike officially began. Forster noted a running theme in his films were emotionally repressed protagonists, and the theme of the picture would be Bond learning to trust after feeling betrayed by Vesper. Forster said he created the Camille character as a strong female counterpart to Bond rather than a casual love interest. She openly shows emotions similar to those which Bond experiences but is unable to express. Haggis located his draft's climax in the Swiss Alps, but Forster wanted the action sequences to be based around the four classical elements of earth, water, air and fire. The decision to homage Goldfinger in Fields's death came about as Forster wanted to show oil had replaced gold as the most precious material. The producers rejected Haggis's idea that Vesper Lynd had a child, because "Bond was an orphan ... Once he finds the kid, Bond can't just leave the kid." The water supply issue in Bolivia was the main theme of the film, with a story based on the Cochabamba Water Revolt.

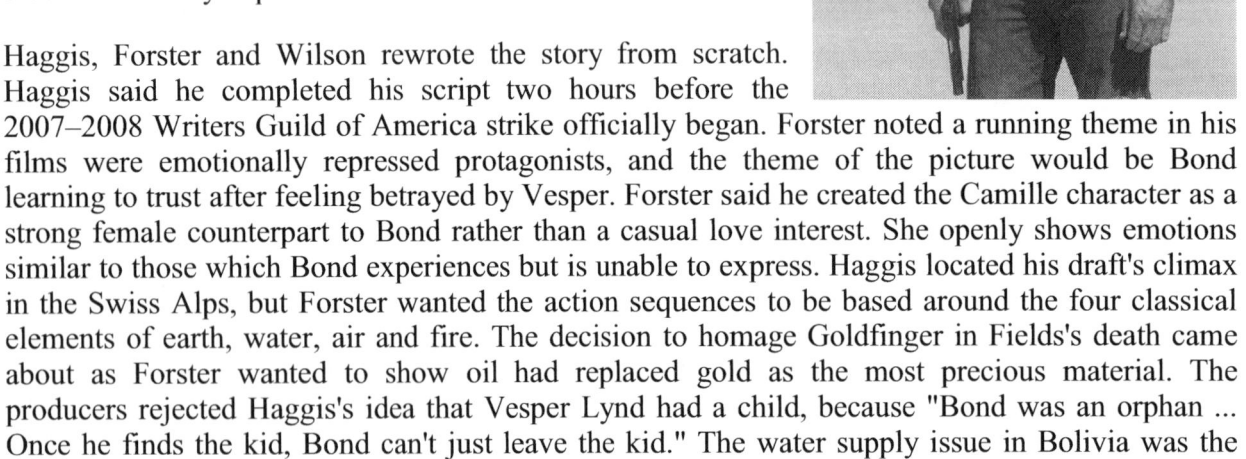

Michael G. Wilson decided on the film's title Quantum of Solace only "a few days" before its announcement on the 24th of January 2008. It was the name of a short story in Ian Fleming's anthology For Your Eyes Only (1960).

During filming, after the Writers Guild strike ended, Forster read a spec script by Joshua Zetumer, which he liked, and hired him to reshape scenes for the later parts of the shoot, which the director was still unsatisfied with. Forster had the actors rehearse their scenes, as he liked to film scenes continually. Zetumer rewrote dialogue depending on the actors' ideas each day.

Quantum of Solace was shot in six countries. Second unit filming began in Italy at the Palio di Siena horse race on August the 16th, 2007, although at that point Forster was unsure how it would fit into the film. Some scenes were filmed also in Maratea and Craco, two small distinctive towns in Basilicata in southern Italy. Other places used for location shooting were Madrid in August, Baja California in Mexico in early 2008 and for shots of the aerial battle; Malcesine, Limone sul Garda and Tremosine in Italy during March, and at Talamone during the end of April. The main unit began on the 3rd of January, 2008 at Pinewood Studios. The 007 Stage was used for the fight in the art gallery, and an MI6 safe house hidden within the city's cisterns, while other stages housed Bond's Bolivian hotel suite, and the MI6 headquarters. Interior and exterior airport scenes were filmed at Farnborough Airfield and the snowy closing scenes were filmed at the Bruneval Barracks in Aldershot.

Shooting in Panama City began on the 7th of February at Howard Air Force Base. The country doubled for Haiti and Bolivia, with the National Institute of Culture of Panama standing in for a hotel in the latter country. A sequence requiring several hundred extras was also shot at nearby Colón. Shooting in Panama was also carried out at Fort Sherman, a former US military base on the Colón coast. Forster was disappointed he could only shoot the boat chase in that harbour, as he had a more spectacular vision for the scene. Officials in the country worked with the locals to "minimise inconvenience" for the cast and crew, and in return hoped the city's exposure in the film would increase tourism. The crew was going to move to Cusco, Peru for ten days of filming on the 2nd of March, but the location was cancelled for budget reasons. Twelve days of filming in Chile began on March the 24th at Antofagasta. There was shooting in Cobija, the Paranal Observatory, and other locations in the Atacama Desert. Forster chose the desert and the observatory's ESO Hotel to represent Bond's rigid emotions, and being on the verge of committing a vengeful act as he confronts Greene in the film's climax.

Marc Forster chose the Atacama Desert to represent Bond's vengefulness in the climax. While filming in Sierra Gorda, Chile, the local mayor, Carlos Lopez, staged a protest because he was angry at the filmmakers' portrayal of the Antofagasta region as part of Bolivia. He was arrested, detained briefly, and put on trial two days later. Eon dismissed his claim that they needed his permission to film in the area. Michael G. Wilson also explained Bolivia was appropriate to the plot, because of the country's history of water problems, and was surprised the two countries disliked each other a century after the War of the Pacific. In a poll by Chilean daily newspaper La Segunda, 75% of its readers disagreed with Lopez's actions, due to the negative image they felt it presented of Chile, and the controversy's potential to put off productions looking to film in the country in the future.

From the 4th to the 12th of April the main unit shot on Sienese rooftops. Shooting on the real rooftops turned out to be less expensive than building them at Pinewood. The next four weeks were scheduled for filming the car chase at Lake Garda and Carrara but this was delayed when, on the 19th of April, an Aston Martin employee driving a DBS to the set crashed into the lake. He survived, and was fined £400 for reckless driving. Another accident occurred two days later when two stuntmen were seriously injured, with one, Greek stuntman Aris Comninos, having to be put in intensive care after his Alfa Romeo collided with another car. Filming of the scenes was temporarily halted so that Italian police could investigate the causes of the accidents. Stunt co-ordinator Gary Powell said the accidents were a testament to the realism of the action. Comninos recovered safely from his injury.

Filming took place at the floating opera stage at Bregenz, Austria, from the 28th of April until the 9th of May. The sequence, where Bond stalks the villains during a performance of Tosca, required 1500 extras. A short driving sequence was filmed at the nearby Feldkirch, Vorarlberg. The crew returned to Italy the following week to shoot a (planned) car crash at the marble quarry in Carrara, and a recreation of the Palio di Siena at the Piazza del Campo in Siena. 1000 extras were hired for a scene where Bond emerges from the Fonte Gaia. Originally, he would have emerged from the city's cisterns at Siena Cathedral, but this was thought disrespectful. By June the crew returned to Pinewood for four weeks, where new sets (including the interior of the hotel in the climax) were built.

Quantum of Solace returned to the traditional gun barrel opening shot, which was altered into part of the story for Casino Royale where it was moved to the beginning of the title sequence. In this film the gun barrel sequence was moved to the end of the movie, which Wilson explained was done for a surprise, and to signify the conclusion of the story begun in the previous film.

Quantum of Solace was the last in Ford Motor's three-film deal that began with 2002's Die Another Day. Although Ford sold over 90% of the Aston Martin Company in 2007, the Aston Martin DBS V12 returned for the film's car chase around Lake Garda. Dan Bradley was hired as second unit director because of his work on the second and third Bourne films, so the film would continue the gritty action style begun in Casino Royale. He had intended to use Ford GTs for the opening chase, but it was replaced by the Alfa Romeo 159. After location filming in Italy, further close-ups of Craig, the cars and the truck were shot at Pinewood against a bluescreen. Originally three Alfa Romeos were in the sequence, but Forster felt the scene was running too long and re-edited the scene so it only looked like two Romeo's were chasing Bond. Six Aston Martins were destroyed during filming, and one of them was purchased by a fan.

Fourteen cameras were used to film the Palio di Siena, footage which was later edited into the main sequence. Aerial shots using helicopters were banned, and the crew were also forbidden from showing any violence "involving either people or animals." To shoot the foot chase in Siena in April of 2008 four camera cranes were built in the town, and a cable camera was also used. Frame store worked on the Siena chase, duplicating the 1000 extras during principal photography to match shots of the 40,000 strong audience at the real Palio, removing wires that held Craig and the stuntmen in the rooftop segment of the chase, and digital expansion of the floor and skylight in the art gallery Bond and Mitchell fall into. The art gallery fight was intended to be simple, but during filming Craig's stunt double accidentally fell from the construction scaffolding. Forster preferred the idea of Bond hanging from ropes reaching for his gun to kill Mitchell.

The Moving Picture Company created the climactic hotel sequence. The fire effects were supervised by Chris Corbould, and post-production MPC had to enhance the sequence by making the smoke look closer to the actors, so it would look more dangerous. A full-scale replica of the building's exterior was used for the exploding part Bond and Camille escape from. The boat chase was another scene that required very little CGI. Machine FX worked on replacing a few shots of visible stuntmen with a digital version of Craig's head, and recreated the boats Bond jumps over on his motorcycle to make it look more dangerous. Crowd creation was done for the Tosca scene by Machine FX, to make the performance look like it had sold out.

Quantum of Solace premiered at the Odeon Leicester Square on the 29th of October, 2008. Princes William and Harry attended, and proceeds from the screening were donated to the charities Help for Heroes and the Royal British Legion. The film was originally scheduled to be released in the UK and North America on the 7th of November; however, Eon pushed forward the British date to the 31st of October during filming, while the American date was pushed back in August to the 14th of November, after Harry Potter and the Half-Blood Prince had been moved to 2009, thereby allowing the distributors to market the film over the autumn blockbuster Thanksgiving holiday weekend. In Australia, the film was moved a week to the 19th of November, after 20th Century Fox chose to release "Australia" on Quantum of Solace's original release date.

Upon its opening in the UK, Quantum of Solace grossed £4.9 million ($8 million), breaking the record for the largest Friday opening in the UK. The film then broke the UK opening weekend record, taking £15.5 million ($25 million) in its first weekend, surpassing the previous record of £14.9 million held by Harry Potter and the Goblet of Fire. It earned a further £14 million in France and Sweden, where it opened on the same day. The weekend gross of the equivalent of $10.6 million in France was a record for the series, surpassing what Casino Royale made in five days by 16%. The $2.7 million gross in Sweden was the fourth-highest opening for a film there.

The following week, the film was playing in sixty countries. It grossed the equivalent of $39.3 million in the UK, $16.5 million in France and $7.7 million in Germany. The film broke records in Switzerland, Finland, United Arab Emirates, Nigeria, Romania and Slovenia. Its Chinese and Indian openings were the second largest ever for foreign-language films.

The film grossed $27 million on its opening day in 3,451 cinemas in Canada and the United States, where it was the number one film for the weekend, with $67.5 million and $19,568 average per cinema. It was the highest-grossing opening weekend Bond film in the U.S., and tied with The Incredibles for the biggest November opening outside of the Harry Potter series. By February of 2010, Quantum of Solace had grossed a total of $586,090,727.

SKYFALL
007
DANIEL CRAIG
JAVIER BARDEM RALPH FIENNES NAOMIE HARRIS BERENICE MARLOHE WITH ALBERT FINNEY AND JUDI DENCH
ANDREW NOAKES DAVID POPE THOMAS NEWMAN JANY TEMIME STUART BAIRD DENNIS GASSNER
ROGER DEAKINS CALLUM McDOUGALL NEAL PURVIS ROBERT WADE AND JOHN LOGAN
MGM
MICHAEL G. WILSON AND BARBARA BROCCOLI SAM MENDES
COLUMBIA PICTURES
OCTOBER 26
Find us on /skyfallmovie

SKYFALL

Production of Skyfall was suspended throughout 2010 because of financial trouble within MGM. It was not until MGM's exit from bankruptcy on the 21st of December, 2010, that production could continue.

After the release of Quantum of Solace in 2008, producer Barbara Broccoli commented that Skyfall, untitled at the time, may continue the plot of the Quantum organisation, introduced in Casino Royale and continued in Quantum of Solace. Ultimately, Skyfall ended up as a stand-alone film.

The main cast of Skyfall was officially announced at a press conference held at the Corinthia Hotel in London on the 3rd of November, 2011, fifty years to the day after Sean Connery was announced to play James Bond in the film Dr. No.

Javier Bardem was cast as the film's principal villain, Raoul Silva, a cyberterrorist who is seeking revenge against those he holds responsible for betraying him. Bardem described Silva as "more than a villain", while Craig stated that Bond has a "very important relationship" to Silva. In casting the role, director Sam Mendes admitted that he lobbied hard for Bardem to accept the part. Mendes saw the potential for the character to be recognised as one of the most memorable characters in the series and wanted to create "something the audience may consider to have been absent from the Bond movies for a long time". He felt that Bardem was one of the few actors up to the task of becoming "colourless" and existing within the world of the film as something more than a function of the plot. In preparing for the role, Bardem had the script translated into his native Spanish to better understand his character, which Mendes cited as being a sign of the actor's commitment to the film. Bardem dyed his hair blond for the role after brainstorming ideas with Mendes to come up with a distinct visual look for the character. Bérénice Marlohe was cast as Séverine, a character who had been saved from the Macau sex trade by Silva and now works as his representative. Marlohe described her character as being "glamorous and enigmatic", and that she drew inspiration from Goldeneye villain Xenia Onatopp.

Ralph Fiennes was cast as Gareth Mallory, a former Lieutenant in the British Army and now the Chairman of the Intelligence and Security Committee, which gives him the authority to regulate MI6. At the end of the film, Mallory becomes the head of MI6, assuming the title of M.

To play the returning character of Miss Moneypenny, Naomi Harris was cast. Harris' role was initially presented as that of Eve, an MI6 field agent who works closely with Bond. Despite ongoing speculation in the media that Harris had been cast as Miss Moneypenny, this was not confirmed by anyone involved in production of the film, with Harris herself even going so far as to dismiss claims that Eve was in fact Moneypenny, stating that "Eve is not remotely office-bound". Another character returning to the series was Q, played by Ben Whishaw.

The producers briefly considered approaching Sean Connery for a cameo in a nod to the 50th anniversary of the film series, but elected not to as they felt Connery's presence would be seen as stunt casting and disengage audiences from the film

Skyfall was directed by Sam Mendes, who first signed on to the project shortly after Quantum of Solace was released, and remained on board as a consultant during the period of uncertainty surrounding MGM's financial situation. Mendes, who had previously worked with Craig on Road to Perdition, was approached after seeing Craig in a production of A Steady Rain. The two met after a performance, where Craig broached the subject of directing a Bond film for the first time. Mendes was at first hesitant to accept the job as directing a Bond film had no appeal to him, but he did not reject the offer immediately because of Craig's involvement and enthusiasm for the project; Mendes described Craig's casting and performance in Casino Royale as being precisely what he felt the Bond franchise needed in its lead actor. He agreed to direct after meeting with Michael G. Wilson and Barbara Broccoli and seeing the early direction the film was going to take.

Peter Morgan was originally commissioned to write a script, but left the project when MGM filed for bankruptcy and production of the film stalled; despite his departure, Morgan later stated that the final script was based on his original idea, retaining what he described as the film's "big hook". Director Mendes adamantly denied this, stating that it was "just not true" and that Morgan's script treatment had been discarded once Mendes agreed to direct. The final script was written by Bond screenwriting regulars Neal Purvis, Robert Wade, and John Logan. Logan recounted being brought into the project by his long-time friend Sam Mendes, describing the process between Mendes and the writers as "very collaborative", and that writing Skyfall was one of the best experiences he had had in scripting a film.

Sam Mendes and Barbara Broccoli travelled to South Africa for location scouting in April of 2011. With the film moving into pre-production in August, plans were made that shooting would take place in India, with scenes to be shot in the Sarojini Nagar district of New Delhi and on railway lines between Goa and Ahmedabad. The production crew faced complications in securing permission to close sections of the Konkan Railway but permission was eventually granted to the Bond production crew; however, the production ultimately did not shoot in India

Principle photography was scheduled to take up 133 days, although the actual filming took 128. Filming began on the 7th of November, 2011, in and around London. Scenes were shot in London Underground stations, Smithfield car park in West Smithfield, the National Gallery, Whitehall, Parliament Square, Charing Cross Station, the Old Royal Navy College, Greenwich, Cadogan Square, Tower Hill, and St. Bartholomew's Hospital. The Old Vic Tunnels underneath Waterloo Station served as the MI6 training grounds. For the meeting between Q and Bond, production worked during the National Gallery's closing hours at night. The Department of Energy and Climate Change was used in the scene when Bond stood on the roof near the end of the film. The Vauxhall Bridge and Millbank was closed to traffic for filming scene where MI6 headquarters explode. Unlike The World is Not Enough, which also featured an explosion at the same building, which was filmed using a large-scale replica the explosion in Skyfall was added digitally in post-production. Shooting of the finale was planned to take place at Duntrune Castle in Argyll, but was cancelled shortly after filming began. Glencoe was instead chosen for filming of these scenes. Although supposedly based in Scotland, Bond's family home of Skyfall was constructed on Hankley Common in Surrey using plywood and plaster to build a full-scale model of the building.

Production moved to Turkey in March, and was expected to take three months in the country. For the fight scene on top of the train and to depict Bond as he is shot and falls from the train, Bond stunt double Andy Lister dived backwards off the 300-foot drop for the scene. A crane was set up on a train carriage to hold a safety line which then caught him. Parts of Istanbul, including the Spice Bazaar, Yeni Camii, the Main Post Office, Sultanahmet Square, and the Grand Bazaar, were closed at various times for filming in April. Store owners in the affected areas were paid around 750 Turkish Lira ($420) per day as compensation.

China was also featured in the film but Bond never actually visited there for Skyfall. Instead, the Virgin Active Pool in London's Canary Wharf acted as Bond's hotel pool in Shanghai, and the entrance to London's fourth tallest building, Broadgate Tower, was also lit up to look like an office building there. For the aerial footage of Shanghai, the crew received rare access to shoot from a helicopter on loan from the Chinese government. The interior of the Golden Dragon Casino in Macau where Bond met Séverine was constructed on a sound stage at Pinewood, with 300 floating lanterns and two 30-foot high dragon heads lighting the set. Additional scenes were filmed with Ascot Racecourse doubling for Shanghai Pudong International Airport.

The premiere of Skyfall was on the 23rd of October, 2012, at the Royal Albert Hall in London. The event was attended by Prince Charles, and his wife Camilla, Duchess of Cornwall. The film was released in the U.K. three days later into US cinemas on the 8th of November. Skyfall was the first Bond film to be screened in IMAX venues and was released into IMAX cinemas in North America a day earlier than the conventional cinema release.

Skyfall has earned $1,108.6 million worldwide, and is the highest-grossing film worldwide for Sony Pictures and the second highest grossing film of 2012. On its opening weekend, it earned $80.6 million from 25 markets and in the U.K. the film grossed £20.1 million on its opening weekend, making it the second-highest Friday-to-Sunday debut ever behind Harry Potter and the Deathly Hallows – Part 2. It also achieved the second-highest IMAX debut ever behind The Dark Knight Rises. The film set a record for the highest seven-day gross with £37.2 million, surpassing previous record holder Deathly Hallows – Part 2 (£35.7 million). By the 9th of November 2012 the film had earned over £57 million to surpass The Dark Knight Rises as the highest-grossing film of

2012, and the highest-grossing James Bond film of all time in the UK. After 40 days of release the total UK gross stood at £94.28 million, making Skyfall the highest grossing film in the U.K, surpassing the £94.03 million of Avatar. By the 30th of December, 2012, it became the first film to gross more than £100 million ($161.6 million) in the UK. Skyfall's takings at the box office saw it become only the fourteenth film and first Bond film to gross over $1,000 million, making it the seventh highest-grossing film ever made at the time and taking it past the inflation-adjusted amount of $1,047 million earned by Thunderball.

In North America, the film opened in 3,505 cinemas, the widest opening for any Bond film. The film earned $2.4 million from midnight showings on its opening day and a further $2.2 million from IMAX and large-format cinemas. Skyfall went on to gross $30.8 million on its opening day in the U.S. and Canada, and $88.4 million in its opening weekend, the biggest debut yet for a Bond film. By the end of its theatrical run, the film earned $304,360,277 in the United States and Canada, making it the fourth highest-grossing film of 2012 in these regions.

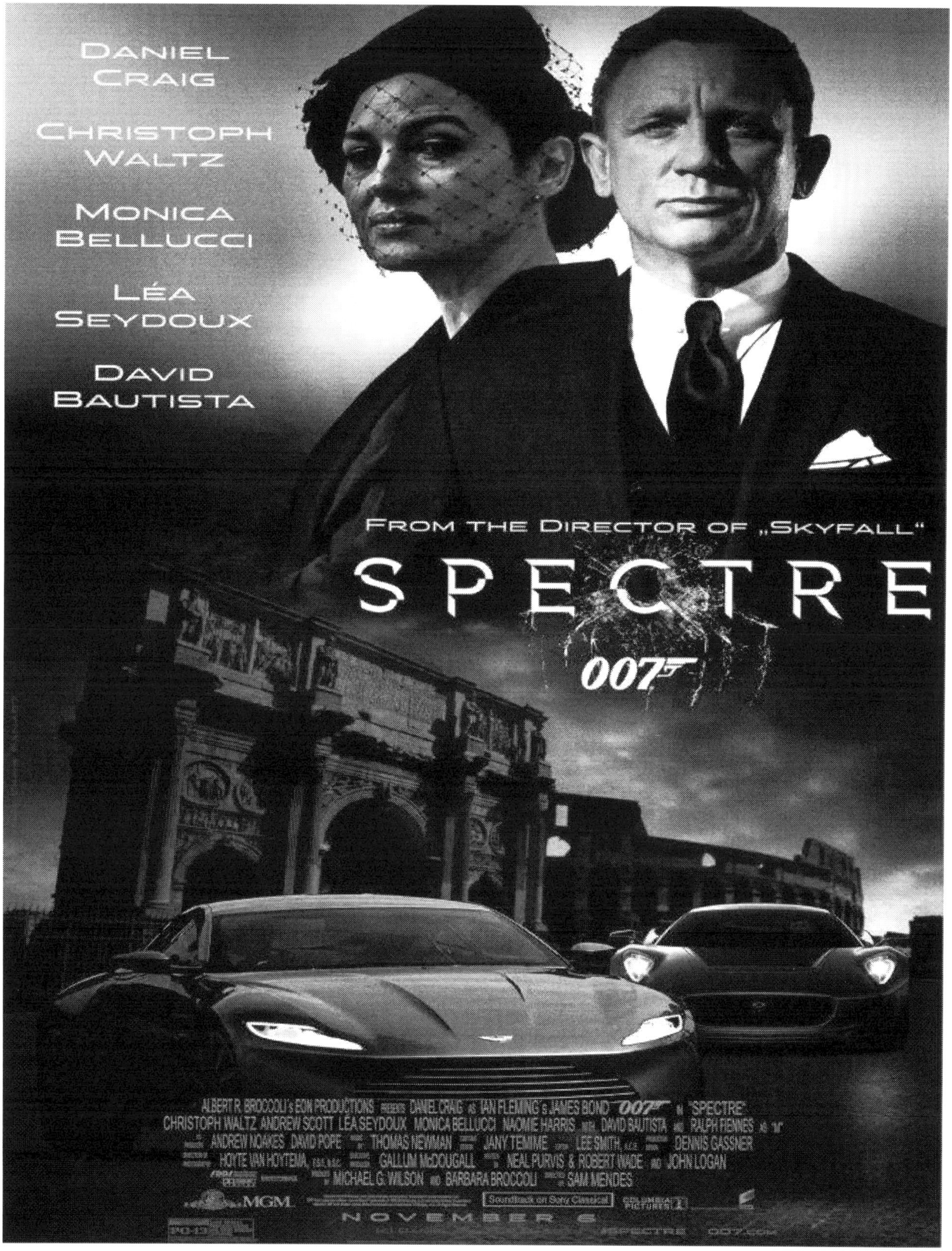
Daniel Craig
Christoph Waltz
Monica Bellucci
Léa Seydoux
David Bautista
From the Director of „Skyfall“
SPECTRE
007
ALBERT R. BROCCOLI's EON PRODUCTIONS DANIEL CRAIG IAN FLEMING's JAMES BOND 007 "SPECTRE"
CHRISTOPH WALTZ ANDREW SCOTT LÉA SEYDOUX MONICA BELLUCCI NAOMIE HARRIS DAVID BAUTISTA RALPH FIENNES "M"
ANDREW NOAKES DAVID POPE THOMAS NEWMAN JANY TEMIME LEE SMITH DENNIS GASSNER
HOYTE VAN HOYTEMA GALLUM McDOUGALL NEAL PURVIS & ROBERT WADE JOHN LOGAN
MICHAEL G. WILSON BARBARA BROCCOLI SAM MENDES
MGM
Soundtrack on Sony Classical
NOVEMBER 6
007.com

SPECTRE

The ownership of the SPECTRE organisation and its characters had been at the centre of long-standing litigation starting way back in 1961 between Ian Fleming and Kevin McClory.

In November of 2013 MGM and the McClory estate formally settled the issue with Danjaq, LLC/Eon Productions and MGM acquired the full copyright film rights to the concept of SPECTRE and all of the characters associated with it. The longstanding feud between McClory and the Bond world appears to have finally come to an end.

Despite being an original story, Spectre draws on Ian Fleming's source material, most notably in the character of Franz Oberhauser, played by Christoph Waltz. Oberhauser shares his name with Hannes Oberhauser, a background character in the short story "Octopussy" from the Octopussy and The Living Daylights collection, and who had been a temporary legal guardian of a young Bond in 1983. Similarly, Charmian Bond is shown to have been his full-time guardian, observing the back story established by Fleming.

The main cast were revealed in December of 2014 at the 007 Stage at Pinewood Studios with Daniel Craig making his fourth appearance as Bond and Ralph Fiennes, Naomi Harris, and Ben Whishaw reprising their roles of M, Eve Moneypenny, and Q.

Christoph Waltz was cast in the role of Franz Oberhauser, though he refused to comment on the nature of the part. Dave Bautista was cast as Mr. Hinx after producers sought an actor with a background in contact sport and Monica Bellucci also joined the cast as Lucia Sciarra, becoming the oldest actor to be cast as a "Bond girl" at the age of fifty. Jesper Christensen also reprises his role as Mr. White from Casino Royale and Quantum of Solace. The character of Mr. White had previously been killed off in a scene intended to be used as an epilogue to Quantum of Solace before it was removed from the final cut of the film, enabling his return in Spectre.

In addition to the principal cast, Alessandro Cremona was cast as Marco Sciarra, Stephanie Sigman was cast as Estrella, and Detlef Bothe was cast as a villain for scenes shot in Austria. In February of 2015 over fifteen hundred extras were hired for the pre-title sequence set in Mexico depicting a huge street carnival. With a small time gap to shoot the street filming, the huge amount of extras had to be dressed, make up applied, and in front of the cameras in a short space of time. The chain of Make-up artists employed for the scene got everybody ready and out in less than 75 minutes.

Sam Mendes had originally said that he would not be returning to direct another Bond but later changed his mind and agreed to take on what was then just titled "Bond 24". Skyfall writer John Logan resumed his role of scriptwriter, collaborating with Neal Purvis and Robert Wade, who returned for their fifth Bond film. The writer Jez Butterworth also worked on the script, alongside Mendes and Daniel Craig had a lot of input.

Production began on the 8th of December, 2014, at Pinewood Studios, with filming taking seven months. Mendes also confirmed several filming locations, including London, Mexico City, and Rome. Early filming took place at Pinewood Studios, and around London, with scenes variously featuring Craig and Harris at Bond's flat, and Craig and Kinnear travelling down the River Thames.

Filming in Austria was taken around Solden, including the Otztal Glacier Road, Rettenback Glacier and the adjacent ski resort and cable car station. Obertilliach and Lake Altaussee were also used. Scenes filmed in Austria centred on the Ice Q Restaurant, standing in for the fictional Hoffler Klinik, a private medical clinic in the Austrian Alps. Filming included an action scene featuring a Land Rover Defender Bigfoot and a Range Rover Sport.

Production was temporarily halted first by an injury to Craig, who sprained his knee whilst shooting a fight scene, and later by an accident involving a filming vehicle that saw three crew members injured, at least one of them seriously.

Filming temporarily returned to England to shoot scenes at Blenheim Palace in Oxfordshire, which stood in for a location in Rome, before moving on to the city itself for a five-week shoot across the city, with locations including the Ponte Sisto bridge and the Roman Forum. The production faced opposition from a variety of special interest groups and city authorities who were concerned about the potential for damage to historical sites around the city and problems with graffiti and rubbish appearing in the film. A car chase scene set along the banks of the Tiber River and through the streets of Rome featured an Bond in his latest Aston Martin DB10 and a Jaguar C-X75. The C-X75 was originally developed as a hybrid electric vehicle with four independent battery-powered engines before the project was cancelled. Jaguar converted the prototype car to use a conventional internal combustion engine for use in the film.

With filming completed in Rome, production moved to Mexico City in late March to shoot the film's opening sequence, with scenes to include the Day of the Dead festival filmed in and around the Zocalo and the Centro Historico district. The planned scenes required the city square to be closed for filming a sequence involving a fight aboard an Messerschmitt-Bolkow-Blohm Bo 150 helicopter flown by stunt pilot Chuck Aaron. The stunt called for modifications to be made to several buildings to prevent damage with the film's second unit moving the helicopter to Palenque in the state of Chiapas to film aerial manoeuvres considered too dangerous to shoot in an urban area.

A brief shoot at London's City Hall was filmed on the 18th of April while Mendes was on location and the following month filming took place on the Thames in London. Stunt Scenes involving Craig and Seydoux on a speedboat as well as a low flying helicopter near Westminster Bridge were shot at night, with filming temporarily closing Westminster and Lambeth Bridges. Scenes were also shot on the river near MI6's headquarters at Vauxhall Cross. The crew returned to the river less than a week later to film scenes solely set on Westminster Bridge. The London Fire Brigade were on set to simulate rain as well as monitor smoke used for filming.

After wrapping up in England, production travelled to Morocco in June, with filming to take place in Oujda, Tangier, and Erfoud after preliminary work is completed by the production's second unit.

With release of Spectre scheduled for November of 2015, we shall see what happens next. It can only be concluded that the film will be as successful, if not more, than the previous. No matter what happens. I fear not that Bond will return in one form or another for another 60 years.

"The spy story to end all spy stories"

--Ian Fleming… And that is exactly what he did.

Collection Editions
Limited Edition Books

collectioneditions.com

Printed in Great Britain
by Amazon.co.uk, Ltd.,
Marston Gate.